The Church Newsletter Handbook

The Church Newsletter Handbook

Clayton A. Lord Jr.

Judson Press ® Valley Forge

The Church Newsletter Handbook
©1997 Judson Press, Valley Forge, PA 19482-0851

Library of Congress Cataloging-in-Publication Data

Lord, Clayton A.
    The church newsletter handbook / Clayton A. Lord, Jr.
        p. cm
    ISBN 0-8170-1248-8 (alk. paper)
    1. Church newsletters—Handbooks, manuals, etc. I. Title,
BV653.3.L67 1997
254'.3—dc21   97-17431

05   04   03   02   01   00   99   98   97

10   9   8   7   6   5   4   3   2   1

Contents

Acknowledgments

I am very aware that nothing we do materializes out of a void, and so it is with this book. The content of this handbook arises out of the experiences of many people involved in God's ministry. It is to some of these who have influenced and taught me over the years that I want to express my gratitude.

First and foremost, I want to thank the members of the First Baptist Church of Norwich, Connecticut, for helping me with this project. Their suggestions and critiques of our church newsletter, as well as comments we received from neighboring congregations, have helped shape this work and the ministry that evolved from it. Many of the newsletters and articles reprinted in the pages of this book are from their ministry.

I also want to thank my wife, Lori, and my three daughters, Rebecca, Sarah, and Rachel, for persevering while I finished this handbook. I give them my word that we will go for ice cream again as soon as this book goes to press.

I would like to thank Amy and George Rezendes for their assistance with this project. Amy was my proofreader and also helped with the typing. George helped me keep my sanity as I was getting everything ready for production and battling a temperamental computer. Thanks also to my secretary, Buffy McFalls, who helped me get through the final stages of production.

I would like to thank Jerry Handspicker for his encouragement as I wrote and rewrote. He helped me find myself in the process. And I want to thank my colleagues in southeastern Connecticut for sharing their knowledge of the subject. Some of their newsletters are lifted up in these pages.

I also want to thank the Andover Newton community, faculty, and administration for providing a place where gifts can be nurtured. This project began as work for the doctor of ministry program.

Finally, this project is dedicated to the memory of my pastor, Rev. Dr. John H. Brooks. He was a teacher like no other—a source of lifelong inspiration.

Introduction

What Inspired This Book?

Twenty-five years ago a pastor came to a small New England town. The pastor, John Brooks, was from Australia and his wife, Janet Brooks, hailed from Seattle, Washington. They were city folks who had traveled a great deal prior to settling down in that rural village. When Janet became ill, John received a lot of support from the congregation. Wanting to return the love that the people had given him, he searched for a way to reach out to the church family and to communicate the sense of community he felt. He chose to do this through a church newsletter. It became an epistle that lifted up the ministry of the people in that church.

In many ways, John Brooks was just reviving an old tradition through his newsletter. He was using the written word to communicate the Good News. The word was expressed in his personal style, and that made it unique. He also described life in that community, and that made it special. I grew up in that church and realized that the church newsletter is a gift that all of us can use to make our ministries more effective.

Why Use the Written Word?

People today have access to more forms of communication than ever before. We can pick up the telephone and talk to family and friends who are halfway around the world; there is hardly a need to write letters anymore. We can turn on the television news and watch an event happen as it takes place; newspapers are out of date even as they go to press. We can turn on the computer and access a network that offers an endless array of entertainment and educational resources; electronic mail allows us to talk to people with similar interests around the world. All of this can be done without moving away from the desk or getting out of the chair.

Even with all this communicating, however, there is something missing; it is the feeling that we belong to a local community. That is why I am writing this book for church leaders. The written word still has a place in the world today. It is poetic and romantic. It opens our imaginations and allows us to become part of the story. It builds community and a sense of history.

I watched John Brooks minister to a congregation by creating a very interesting and very personal newsletter. He shared his thoughts about the ministry and the people who served God in that community, and he made us all feel a part of what was happening in the church.

The apostle Paul used epistles to share his vision of ministry with the churches. The Gospel writers used the written word to preserve the Good News of Jesus Christ. Today, we can continue to use this tradition to reach new people with the gospel. This handbook is intended to serve you and your ministry by helping you produce and distribute better newsletters.

As Christians, we know that better than anyone. We are a people who live by a Book. The early church leaders shared their experiences and then wrote them down so that they could be preserved. Those writings were circulated and shared among the various communities, and all took courage and strength from what they read. As the written records were gathered together, the Book went to places where those early Christians could not go. All who read it then and have read it since have received the Good News.

As we write our stories today, we can tell them in a way that will inspire and give hope to the next generation growing up in our own faith communities. We can recapture the excitement by bringing the Good News to life again through the written word.

We can do this in our church newsletters. We now have technology at our disposal that enables us to produce publications that are better than ever before. We can share what is happening and draw back those who have drifted away from church life. We can build community and preserve a sense of history for those who know us best. All it takes is a little time and a willingness to look at what is new and to take another look at something we used to do so well.

How to Use This Book

This handbook is for pastors, church secretaries, and active laypeople who are engaged in the ministry of producing church bulletins and newsletters.

Some people reading this book may just be getting started. They want to know what equipment they need, what to write, and how to get information for the newsletters. Chapters 1–3 are written with them in mind. Chapters 12–14 also discuss some basic aspects of newsletter production.

Chapters 4–9 include suggestions for those with some experience who are looking for ways to improve their work. Thoughts are shared about layout, typeface, column formatting, and the use of graphics and illustrations. There are also tips on how to write and shape articles for easier reading.

For readers who feel comfortable with their present layout and design, chapters 10-11 offer some ideas that help bring a page to life. Also along these lines, chapter 3 offers some suggestions on different story ideas.

This handbook consists of fourteen short chapters. It is set up like a cookbook for newsletter writers. The chapters are clearly identified and laid out so that the book models the design and format that it suggests for the newsletter editor. So read and write on!

Why Do You Want to Publish a Church Newsletter?

What Is a Newsletter?

Everyone knows what a newsletter is. We have all read one at some time in our lives. Most people belong to clubs and organizations that publish newsletters for their memberships. These written epistles are read and then filed away. We take these publications for granted because they are so familiar. But if we want to produce better newsletters, we need to have a clear understanding of what they are.

Quite simply, a newsletter is a written collection of news stories, notes, and editorials that arise out of the life of an organization. Like the local newspaper, an organization's newsletter is distributed regularly to a specific audience with information that will interest, enrich, and empower it. The articles are timely and contain something of value to the reader.

Although all newsletters share some common elements, each differs from all the others in a number of ways. These differences stem primarily from two factors: (1) the organization's goal in writing the newsletter and (2) the audience to which it is written.

Stating Your Mission

The primary purpose of any newsletter is to inform, invite, and inspire its readers to take an action or a stand on behalf of the organization that publishes it. Therefore, the most effective newsletter editors begin the process of writing with the typewriter covered or the computer turned off. Good newsletter production begins with a statement of purpose. This statement answers the question, What is the organization's main purpose or mission and how can the newsletter help accomplish that?

Many newsletter editors never get around to addressing this matter specifically. When producing their masterpieces, they get caught up in the creative aspect of designing the newsletter and simply forget who they are, who their audience is, and what they are trying to say.

As a church newsletter editor, you will want to state what your church does as your starting point. A typical list of church ministries might look like this:

Newsletters come in all shapes and sizes, but they have one thing in common: They share news and information about the organization that creates them. Like a newspaper, they bring timely articles that reach out to a targeted group of readers.

Our church

- preaches the good news,
- teaches the commandments,
- builds up a community of faith,
- develops a ministry of prayer,
- equips the saints for ministry,
- proclaims peace and justice, and
- ministers to the sick and dying.

After developing your own list of ministries, it is time to look for ways that the newsletter can help you accomplish these purposes. As you find ways to use the newsletter to meet the needs of your ministry, write them down. This will form the basis of the mission statement for the newsletter.

Frame a copy of the mission statement and display it so that you can see it whenever you work on the newsletter. This will help shape the design and content of the publication you are creating.

Our Church Newsletter Mission

- *We will use it to provide a lifeline to everyone in the parish.*
- *We will use it to share the gospel through brief meditations.*
- *We will use it to encourage and uplift the sick and the shut-in.*
- *We will use it to teach doctrinal truths.*
- *We will use it to foster a community of prayer.*
- *We will use it as one vehicle for sharing a vision of the church and its ministry to the community.*
- *We will use it as one way to introduce new programs to the whole community.*
- *We will use it to promote and advertise the church.*
- *We will use it to build a community of love and understanding.*

Defining Your Audience

The next step in the process of producing a newsletter is identifying your audience. You do this by thinking about the people who will be reading the newsletter.

As a church newsletter editor, you will want to have a mental picture of the people who will be reading your publication.

The first step here is getting specific: who are the readers? Name a few of them and then ask the following questions:

- What is their interest in the church?
- What do they need to know about church activities?
- What else is happening in their lives?
- How old are they? What are their special needs?
- Do they have families or do they live alone?
- What would excite and inspire them to action?
- What is the best way to get their attention?

It is important to remember that even within a fairly homogeneous church group, there are differences in age, education, theological perspective, and socioeconomic status. Recognizing these differences will affect the way you will present your material.

A second step in defining the audience is to name the different groups that make up the intended readership.

Your list might include older adults, young families, teenagers, shut-ins, interested nonmembers, nonattending members, extended family of members, single parents, college students, and so on.

The people on this list will help you fashion and focus what goes into the newsletter. For example, a newsletter for a church with many older members will want to use large print to make reading easier. A newsletter for a church with a large number of families with young children is well advised to present more articles geared toward parenting. Pages or articles for children may also be a part of the package.

If the newsletter is used as a means of evangelism and outreach to new members, it needs to be stripped of "insider references." Everything that is mentioned will have to be spelled out. If you are writing for shut-ins or nonattending members, you might share more news about what has happened so they can picture it clearly.

The reason for this planning is simple. People are extremely busy today. Their lives are filled with activity, and their schedules are overloaded. Many people are hurting as families struggle to survive the ups and downs of the economy. As you think of the people you are writing to, your focus will become sharper and your writing will be more clearly defined. You will be better able to reach out to them and accomplish your mission.

Your Church Ambassador

Finally, the church newsletter is an ambassador for the church and its ministry. It brings good tidings to the reader. It reaches people and places that might be otherwise missed. In truth, the newsletter will probably reach more people at one time than anything else you do.

The people who receive the newsletter will welcome it as an expression of your interest in them. They will read it to find out what your church is doing and to gain an understanding of who your people are and what is important to them.

People seeing the newsletter for the

Ambassadorial Positions

Make a list of all the people connected to the church right now. Then add the names of people who need to know more about the church. Finally, write down those people or organizations who should hear about what you are doing. Broaden the base of your exposure, and word of your work will get out.

A newsletter can be a valuable asset in building up and promoting your church ministry. Share your vision and your good work and let the world know what you are doing. Matthew, one of the first church writers, reminds us in chapter 5 of his Gospel that we are the salt of the earth and the light of the world. Don't hide what you are doing. Tell about it in the pages of your newsletter and let God use your writing to build up your ministry.

Local Embassies

1. Active church families
2. Shut-in and infirm members
3. Active nonmembers
4. College students
5. Winter or summer regulars
6. Visitors
7. New neighbors
8. Church employees

General Embassies

1. Denominational officials
2. Former ministers
3. Interested former members
4. Interested relatives of members
5. Local colleges and seminaries

Community Embassies

1. City officials
2. School officials
3. Newspaper editors
4. People with whom you do business
5. Service agencies
6. Radio and television stations
7. Other local churches and synagogues
8. Community leaders
9. Leaders of groups who use your church facility

Let your newsletter represent your ministry in these places and in any other areas where it can build rapport in your community.

first time will get a glimpse of community life at your church and form an opinion about whether they like it or not. First impressions are important, and that is the primary reason for investing so much time and energy in designing, writing, and distributing your newsletter. It can truly enhance your ministry and your outreach.

Many churches do not advertise themselves, but a newsletter can function to promote the church and its ministry. It can project an image of the church. If you work at it, you can use this to your advantage and put together a newsletter that truly shares a picture of your ministry at its best. Highlight the strengths of its ministry and

The good news for writers of church newsletters is this: your publication will enjoy a broad readership. Surveys among local and national denominational churches have shown that a vast majority of those who receive church newsletters read at least part of them.

honestly evaluate its weaknesses. Show the audience that you are engaged and active, and you will project an active ministry. Emphasize the programs and how they relate to individual needs, and you will touch people where they are. Let the news in the newsletter tell what you are doing, and it will speak for your ministry in a way that no one person can.

Send this good news to as many people as you can. Cost is always a consideration, but the more goodwill your church newsletter promotes, the stronger the platform your ministry has in your community. Send it to present church members and attenders, but do not stop there. Send it to church neighbors, former members, friends, community officials, and anyone else who might have the slightest interest in what you are doing. Let the newsletter be your representative in the community by reaching people you may not see on a regular basis. Let them know the church is alive and active. Sharing this good news might just start a revival for the whole congregation.

Conclusion

Why do you want a church newsletter? The answer is simple: because it will enhance and strengthen your present ministry.

- Church newsletters are considered trustworthy and are widely read by members.
- Church newsletters inform, invite, and inspire members into action.
- Church newsletters build a sense of community among the members and friends of the church.
- Church newsletters promote and advertise your ministry to those who do not know you.
- Church newsletters help focus and direct the church's mission by providing a platform to build on.
- Church newsletters go to a significant number of people at one time and make it possible to accomplish more as a result.

What You Need To Get Started

The Tools of the Trade

Good news awaits those who have never produced a church newsletter before. Every church office already has the equipment it needs to start publishing a newsletter. You do not need to wait until you can afford a computer or a word processor. You can start your first edition using only a typewriter and a mimeograph or a copy machine.

You need five basic tools to produce a church newsletter:

- A vehicle for setting the type, such as a typewriter, a word processor, or a computer.

- Layout or style sheets to help set up the page. They can be used manually with typewriters, and they are included in computer software designed for this purpose.

- Rulers, scissors, glue sticks, and basic office supplies to make the straight lines, cut out the illustrations, and aid in pasting up the pages.

- Volunteer or paid staff to assist in gathering news and getting the newsletter out to the public.

- A machine to duplicate the newsletter.

Setting the Type

Since the predominant element in a newsletter is the printed word, the type will be the most prominent feature. There are several ways to set the type.

Using a Typewriter

The typewriter is standard equipment in most church offices, and it can be used to produce a good newsletter. Typewriters can give a professional look and a typeset appearance. Older typewriters have only one typeface and one size of type, but most newer models allow you to choose from three sizes (from largest to smallest): pica (10 pitch), elite (12 pitch), and micro (15 pitch). The larger the pitch number, the more characters will fit per inch on the page. For example, ten letters fit within an inch with pica, whereas fifteen characters fit within an inch with micro. So, even a newsletter produced on a typewriter can vary its appearance.

Up until ten years ago, most churches had little choice in how they prepared their church publications. The typewriter was standard equipment, and everything was produced on the mimeograph machine or by cutting and pasting pieces together and then running them off on a copy machine.

Some typewriters allow you to vary the type by changing the little metal ball or print wheel that prints the characters on the page. These balls and wheels spin and rotate to stamp the letters. When you want to change to a different typeface, you simply snap in a different ball or wheel.

Using a Word Processor

A word processor makes typing the newsletter easier for many people. Laying out a page and making corrections also require less time when using a word processor. Most word processors have built-in margin settings that make design simpler for the novice. The best feature of these machines comes into play in the editing and rewriting phase of producing the newsletter. The word processor memory remembers what has been typed, so the editor can go back and rewrite a paragraph or more of what has previously been written. The editor can correct mistakes and rework a section without having to start from scratch each time.

The word processor also has two other features that make it an improvement over the typewriter. First, it can use proportional spacing. This means that each letter gets a proportional amount of space based on the size of the character. For example, a *w* would get more space than an *i* because the *w* is bigger. In contrast, a typewriter gives them both the same amount of space, so that every *w* looks smaller than every *i*. This slows the movement of the reader's eyes across the page. Second, a word processor can justify text or center it on a page. (Justifying text causes the words to be spread out evenly across a line.)

More advanced word processors actually help design and lay out pages, and they use floppy disks to store information, just as most computers do. They can be useful to the novice who is just getting into desktop publishing at the church.

One final feature that appeals to many clerical workers is the spell checker. It identifies spelling errors and corrects them long before they reach the printed page. (It will not, however, catch misplaced or misused words that are spelled correctly. Proofreading, therefore, is always an essential step in the production of a newsletter.)

Using a Personal Computer

The personal computer, with its array of desktop publishing programs, is the newest and best means of producing newsletters. Many churches have already made the leap into the computer age.

The computer costs more than either the typewriter or the word processor because the hardware (the computer), the software (the programs), and especially additional libraries of clip art and fonts (typefaces), have to be purchased. The computer allows one person to do almost everything—typing, layout, and placement of illustrations and photographs on the page. Everything is in place before the first copy is printed. There is little or no paste-up.

There are many brands of personal computers on the market today but there are two major operating systems that run them. Personal computers (PCs), also known as IBM compatibles, were pioneered by IBM and later developed by Compaq and other companies. Apple Computers

---

Text justification began with the introduction of the word processor, which utilized new technology to fit the text into certain spatial limitations. Justified text allows the reader to anticipate words and spaces, and some scholars argue that it makes reading easier.

This text is set in the justified format, whereas the text to the right has a ragged right edge. Which do you like better?

The personal computer burst onto the marketplace in 1975. Apple, Kaypro, and Morrow began producing personal microprocessors.

In 1984 IBM got involved with the PC AT and started a revolution. In the same year Apple released the Macintosh 512, and the world has never been the same. Even today, no one is certain where the computer market is going, but one thing is for sure: the computer is here to stay.

developed the Macintosh computer, commonly referred to as a Mac.

Over the last decade, people have debated the relative quality of PCs and Macs. PCs tend to be less expensive, and more software is available for them. The Macs are easier to learn to use, but they cost more, and software for them is more difficult to find.

If you are considering buying a new computer, remember this: whatever computer you now have is best as long as it does what you want it to do. There is no learning curve involved. If you do not have a computer, remember this: if you have someone in the congregation who knows computers and is willing to help you, that person's favorite brand should be your favorite brand.

A computer is a wonderful tool, and it can be used in many aspects of ministry. It can make life easier for the minister and the church staff, especially when it comes to producing the newsletter.

The important features to look for in a computer are the central processing unit (CPU), hard disk drive, floppy disk drive, random access memory (RAM), and the software program that best suits your needs. A minimally adequate computer configuration should include the following:

- 486DX2/66 processor
- 850-megabyte hard disk drive
- 1.44-megabyte floppy disk drive
- 8 megabytes of RAM
- SVGA monitor (0.39 or smaller dot pitch; 0.28 is preferable)
- Mouse
- Windows 3.1 or Windows 95
- Printer

Most desktop publishing programs demand a lot of RAM (random access memory). The RAM is the short-term operating memory of the computer. It works only when the computer is turned on, and it allows you to work on a document without saving it every few seconds. Most computers come with a minimum amount of RAM, but you can add more later on.

Graphics and illustrations use a lot of RAM and take up a lot of storage space on the hard disk. A computer needs at least 8 MB (megabytes) of

---

Mac vs. PC:

The real question is: Who will help you when you have a problem? Unless you like reading computer manuals or have a lot of spare time to take classes, find someone who knows about computers to hold your hand as you learn. If the computer expert in your congregation knows one system or the other, go with his or her experience.

RAM and 850 MB of hard disk space to integrate graphics smoothly into a newsletter. You can get by with less of each, but your graphics capacity will be restricted.

There is a lot of software currently on the market, but every program is not compatible with every computer. If you do not already have a computer, choose the best software for your purposes and then purchase a computer that can run that software.

Setting Up the Page

After you have set up your basic equipment, there are a few more tools that you need to design and lay out your newsletters and church publications. These include layout sheets and rulers.

Layout sheets are very helpful if you are working on a typewriter or a word processor. The best ones have the blue, nonreproducible lines to use as a grid. The layout sheets show where the text and graphics are going to lie on the page. They provide the margins and spatial design that you will be working with.

These sheets can be placed under the copy as it is being typed, or text

The old saying "two heads are better than one" is especially true when it comes to producing a newsletter. The most important step in producing a good church newsletter is recruiting volunteers to help with writing and production.

can be cut and pasted to fit over them.

Layout sheets help define the overall look of your publication. You can use one of many formats. You can combine two or three columns into one larger one for variety. The layout sheets are relatively inexpensive, and they can help you achieve a professional look.

Rulers help make straight lines and boxes. Obtain a good metal ruler to use with an X-acto knife and a clear one for lining text. If you have a drafting table, you might consider getting a T-square to help with the lines also.

You do not need the layout sheets if you are working on a computer or a word processor, but you still need rulers, scissors, and X-acto knives for drawing lines and cutting out illustrations. Unless all of your clip art is on disk, you will need glue sticks, rubber cement, and a roller to apply the clip art to the page.

Most desktop publishing applications come complete with sample layouts

and built-in grids. These packages range in price from $40 for a very simple one to $900 for one with professional capabilities. Most churches would be comfortable with something that falls somewhere in between.

The most popular programs now on the market are:

- Quark Xpress
- Aldus PageMaker
- Ventura Publisher
- Ragtime
- Canvas
- Ready Set Go!
- Springboard Publisher
- Timeworks Publish It!
- Aldus Personal Press
- Microsoft Publisher

Setting Up a Newsletter Staff

The staff is probably the single most important element in the production of a regular church newsletter. One person can do a good job, but several people working together can do a great job.

Most churches already have an untapped newsletter staff sitting in the pews. All it takes to get a newsletter off the ground is a few willing volunteers who can give their time, energy, and enthusiasm to the project.

Various roles are available to those who want to help. Some of them require special gifts, while others call for a labor of love. A typical newsletter staff includes the following roles: editor, reporter, information gatherer, office assistant, proofreader, and photographer. These can be paid or volunteer positions. The important thing to remember is that putting together a newsletter is a team effort. Everyone needs to work together to accomplish the task and produce a fine newsletter.

An All-Star News Staff

The editor bears responsibility for the newsletter. The editor recruits volunteers and assigns responsibilities. All decisions on content, layout, and design will rest with the editor as well.

Reporters gather news and information and write the stories that go into the newsletter. A good editor will raise questions that will help writers get their message across to the reader.

Information gatherers can provide the particulars about events but may feel uncomfortable with writing the article. They feed their information to the reporters for the write-up.

Office assistants help with production tasks, including typing, duplicating, folding, labeling, and mailing. This is an area where many hands make light work. These people's efforts need to be appreciated and recognized.

Proofreaders are essential in the production process. They look for obvious and not-so-obvious errors and eliminate them before the newsletter is reproduced.

Photographers and artists have special gifts that can add depth and interest to the newsletters. They take the pictures and develop the artwork that can make the newsletter really jump off the page.

All of these positions can be filled by volunteers who are looking for ways to get involved in ministry. Use them and celebrate their talents.

Setting Up for Reproduction

One copy of a newsletter will not suffice to build and strengthen ministry. You need to reproduce the newsletter and get it into the hands of your reading public. All churches have the means to get this done.

A congregation with limited resources can take camera-ready copy to a print shop and have it run off on a copy machine. Many churches have mimeograph machines that can be used to run off inexpensive copies of newsletters. Other churches have their own copy machines that can produce professional-looking newsletters. Whatever method you use, make sure the copies come out clean and crisp. Saving a few pennies at the end of the production process, if it results in smudged or illegible newsletters, could end up subverting your entire effort.

Conclusion

Most churches already have everything they need to produce a good newsletter. After you get started, you may want to invest in additional equipment, but it is not necessary in the beginning. All you really need to get started is:

- something to set the type, such as a typewriter, a word processor, or a computer;

- a few tools to help you lay out and design the page, like style sheets for the typewriter or a desktop publishing program for the computer;

- some basic office supplies like tape, scissors, rulers, and glue sticks for pasting up your final drafts;

- a few volunteers to help write, prepare, and produce the newsletter; and

- a way to copy your newsletter so that you can supply one to every person in your audience.

Once you have these things in place, you are only hours away from your first edition.

Cost should not prevent anyone from producing a newsletter. You can produce one very inexpensively by using what you have.

Planning for Success in Ministry

Planning Is the First Step

"Prior planning prevents poor performance."

This axiom is as true for newsletter production as it is for other areas of life. If you want to produce a newsletter that people will take the time to read, you have to plan ahead.

Frequency of Mailing

Will your newsletter be a weekly, monthly, or bimonthly publication? What you decide will depend partly on your goal or mission statement. What do you hope to accomplish with the newsletter? Do you want to announce upcoming programs? Do you want to report on happenings in your church community? Do you want to use the newsletter as a teaching tool? Will it be a parish-to-person epistle? Your answers to these questions will help you decide how often you need to publish your newsletter in order to achieve your goals.

Number of Pages

A general rule is that the number of pages grows with the length of the

interval between editions. A weekly publication shares timely information as it happens. A bimonthly or monthly newsletter covers much more ground.

It is important to bear in mind that the average American's attention span has diminished over the years, and people are not willing to spend a lot of time reading a long, wordy document. If the newsletter gives the appearance of needing more than a few minutes to be read, the average person will put it aside.

Content

What stories or announcements will be included in each issue, and who will be responsible for writing or designing that part of the newsletter?

Assignments have to be made and deadlines need to be set to ensure that articles are ready when the stories should be laid out. It is the content that defines your mission, so this is a critical area in the planning process.

Deadlines

It is important to set a regular publication deadline and stick to it.

Many churches send out a monthly newsletter that arrives in the mailbox on the first of each month. The purpose of these monthly mailings is to invite people to come to church programs.

Always keep your readers in mind. Both the length and the content of the newsletter need to be tailored to your particular audience.

Make up a planning sheet and set deadlines for the submission of articles and the retrieval of photographs. Set a date for editing, proofing, and layout for each edition and then stick to it.

A planning sheet will help you avoid becoming rushed as you produce the newsletter. It will improve the quality of the production and the working relationships among your news staffers. You might like the planning sheet shown below.

How you plan is not as important as the fact that you plan. Arrange to do everything in a way that will produce the result you desire. Then put dates next to each event, working backward from the date you want to get the newsletter out. Arrange to have your volunteers ready and then go for it.

A Newsletter That Enhances Your Church's Ministry

You have already defined your purpose in ministry and your goals for the newsletter. Now it is time to get concrete. How is this newsletter going to enhance your ministry? How do you decide what kind of articles to include in it?

The answers are up to you, and your options are limitless. The following types of articles can help you build a more successful ministry through your newsletter:

News of church events. It may seem obvious, but it is important to share what has been happening at church. Have your reporters briefly share highlights of programs, services, and special events.

Member profiles. Short biographical articles featuring different members of the congregation are always well received. You can feature both new members and longtime members to help people get acquainted with each other.

Student news. Including stories about children and what they are doing in church school or in public school is a way to recognize young people and make them (and their parents) feel that they are important to the church family.

People news. Relate the various activities, travels, honors, and interests of families in the congregation. This is a great discussion starter for coffee hour.

Birth announcements. Celebrate one of the most precious moments in the lives of church families. Birth announcements also serve to make new parents feel welcome in the church.

Memorial notices. Minister to families in their time of need as well as lift up in remembrance a life of faithful Christian service.

Announcements of upcoming events. The newsletter is a wonderful way to announce upcoming events and programs. Adding artistic design to the announcements can help build enthusiasm for your activities.

Articles	Person responsible	Articles due	Photos & graphics	Edit & proof	Layout & design	Copyfit as needed	Camera-ready copy	Print copies	Address & mail
Upcoming Events	Bob	12/15	12/18	12/21	12/21	1/3	1/5	1/5	1/6
Christmas Eve	Mary	12/27	12/30	1/2	1/2	1/3	1/5	1/5	1/6
New Year's Celebration	Sue	1/2	1/2	1/2	1/2	1/3	1/5	1/5	1/6
People News	Mary	12/15	12/18	12/21	12/21	1/3	1/5	1/5	1/6
Prayer Corner	Bob	12/27	12/30	1/2	1/3	1/3	1/5	1/5	1/6
Habitat Mission	Henry	12/15	12/18	12/21	12/21	1/3	1/5	1/5	1/6

Deadlines allow your staff to know what to expect, and they help the procrastinator get the job done. Putting together the first few issues will give you a fairly good idea of the time involved in each step of the process. Make up a production sheet and use it to keep everyone on schedule.

Pastor's column. This is a standard feature in most newsletters, but you can work with the pastor to make it something extra special. Try using it as something more than another pulpit.

Financial reports. Share news about church finances and take the opportunity to discuss the meaning of stewardship and service.

Thank-you notes. Publicly thank those who have helped by giving their time, energy, and enthusiasm to the ministry. Thanking people publicly tells the whole congregation that you value their efforts.

Monthly calendar. More and more churches are using calendars, as opposed to lists, to note meetings, events, and services. Many churches include birthdays and anniversaries on this pullout calendar.

Matters of faith and practice. The theological and dogmatic reasons for church practices can be shared in the newsletter.

Inspirational thoughts. Offer readers poems, meditations, and other readings that have inspired you.

Letters from friends. Share notes from former members and nonresident members.

Changes of address. This seems mundane, but it is a real service to those who like to keep in touch with friends and who like to send greeting cards.

Mission news. Relaying stories of what the church is doing on the mission field can help readers identify with the work of the church and the denomination.

Letters to the editor. Encourage members to share thoughts and ideas with each other on an editorial page.

Church history. Help members learn a little history and gain an understanding of the past.

Minutes of important meetings. Share highlights of the meeting, including any decisions that were made.

Cartoons. People like humorous cartoons and will search the newsletter for them. Vary their placement in the newsletter to encourage people to look through it.

Humorous anecdotes. Stories and jokes add color to the newsletter. People look for light reading to help lift the seriousness of life.

News from other churches, the denominational board, and the local community. You can share what is happening in the wider fellowship and offer opportunities for service elsewhere in the community.

Start a file of newsletters from other churches and organizations and look at what they are reporting. See if you can identify their goals. Then see if you can gain any useful ideas.

Newsletter Writer's Report Form

Name of Reporter _____

Name of Event _____ Date of Event _____

Sponsoring Group_____

Thank you for your help in writing this story for our church newsletter. You are making a valuable contribution to the life of our congregation with your time and effort. Please have this story information to the church office as soon as possible. Please remember that our monthly deadline is the last Friday of the month.

Who is (was) in charge?

What is (was) the occasion?

Who is (was) invited?

Are (were) there any special guests?

List the significant happenings during the event.

Get the reaction of five people to the event.

1.

2.

3.

4.

5.

Is there any important information that would enhance the story?

Were any people singled out for their efforts and why?

Your phone number _____

Many people say the hardest part of producing a newsletter is getting the articles written and delivered before the deadline. Help your writers by giving them a form that they can use to organize their thoughts and keep track of the facts.

Getting the Stories You Want before the Deadline

If you make it easy to report the news, you will have greater success in recruiting reporters and getting stories in hand before the deadline. Most newsletter staffs are made up of dedicated volunteers who receive little or no pay. Their time and energy is limited, and a form that helps them pull together the information that you want will help them write their reports more efficiently.

Every reporter and story writer should take such a form to any events they attend. It will guide them in jotting down particulars and asking questions that will help flesh out the story. Then they can write their own stories, or they can have someone else write them.

Conclusion

Planning ahead makes the difference between a very good newsletter and an average one. The process begins with choosing what you will report and ends with getting your newsletter to the post office. Listed below are the steps to follow in producing a monthly newsletter.

1. **Choose the stories** or articles that will go into the newsletter this issue.

2. **Appoint the reporters** and give them the report forms and suggestions on the stories you want.

3. **Lay out your pages** with a guess on space for each story. This will be a rough layout.

4. **Choose your graphics** and plan your photographs and put them in the rough layout.

5. **Collect the stories** and articles from the reporters and begin fitting them into your layout.

6. **Edit the stories** and check spelling. Have a third person proofread the newsletter.

7. **Prepare the final camera-ready copy** and get it ready for production.

8. **Reproduce the newsletter** for the mailing audience.

9. **Address and mail** the newsletters.

Giving the Newsletter That Special Appeal

Capturing Your Reader's Attention

Everybody is busy. The demands on people's time and attention are enormous. And the people we are trying to reach with our church newsletters are no different.

Solicitors fill our mailboxes with an endless barrage of letters, leaflets, brochures . . . you name it. We must choose which pieces of mail we read immediately, which pieces we read later, and which pieces we file.

Thus a newsletter's appearance is all-important. If it is designed so that it shouts "**READ ME**," parishioners are likely to look through it right away rather than putting it aside for later perusal.

Make a file of the assorted mail that turns up in your mailbox. Which pieces catch your attention? Why? Study the most effective pieces for styles and designs that you can adapt to your newsletter. Good design is important. It is an elaboration of your communication skills since it emphasizes and punctuates your message. Poor design will negate anything you write.

Look at the newsletters on the next page. What strikes you about each one? What elements are most effective in attracting your attention? Now look at your newsletter and ask the same questions. Would it stand out in a mailbox? In the next few pages we will examine graphic designs that grab a reader's attention.

Three Categories of Mail

Most people divide the mail they find in their mailboxes into three categories. The first category is "must open." Personal letters and expected messages fall into this group. People look forward to receiving them and drop everything else to open them. Just think about it for a moment. What do you open first when you go to the mailbox? If we want people to read our newsletters right away, we need to deliver something that speaks to readers personally.

A second category is "important to keep." Monthly bills and important papers fall into this category. This kind

Many people have a special relationship with the mailbox. It can be the source of great joy or the harbinger of bad news. When designing our church newsletter, we should make it as warm and inviting as possible so that people will actually look forward to receiving it.

of mail may not be opened right away, but it is saved for future attention. It does not end up stuck between the seat cushions or lost in the utility room. It is put in a safe place. A lot of church newsletters fall into this category. We offer people information that they need, but it is not urgent enough to be included in the exciting pile. This is where layout can make a difference. A well-designed newsletter can catch the reader's attention and focus it on the news and information that we want to communicate to them.

The last category is "look at it later." Catalogues, special offers, ads, and unsolicited mail falls here. Mail in this pile will be attended to when there is nothing more important to do. People are not as careful with it. It often gets lost, and most of it ends up in the wastebasket. A church newsletter that looks like a government notice will find its way into this pile. Has anyone ever complained of not hearing about an event at church? This could tell you that your newsletter ended up in this third category.

The editor's goal is to move the newsletter from the third category to the first so that our message has the best opportunity of being received and acted on. This is why the time spent on layout and design is so important.

Pick up newsletters from other churches and consider what they are doing. It will help you decide what is appealing and what is not. Look at the mail you receive from other sources and take notes. What grabs your attention?

Elements of Newsletter Design

The artistic ability that produces good design is often thought of as a gift, not something that can be learned. As a result, a lot of people feel they cannot "do" design and layout. But good design actually results from the knowledge of a few basics in graphic design.

Good newsletter design begins with columns, margins and white space, text, rules, boxes, headlines, graphics, and photographs. It continues with unity and consistency throughout the document.

Nameplate

Logo

Dateline

Major Headline

Photograph

Body Text

Caption

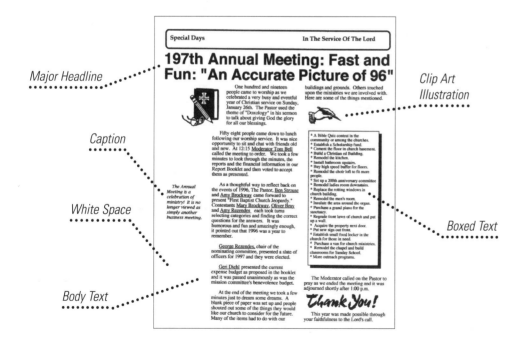

Major Headline

Caption

White Space

Body Text

Clip Art Illustration

Boxed Text

Two Column
Format

Kicker

Major Headline

White Space

Return Address

Pull quote

Indicia

Address Panel

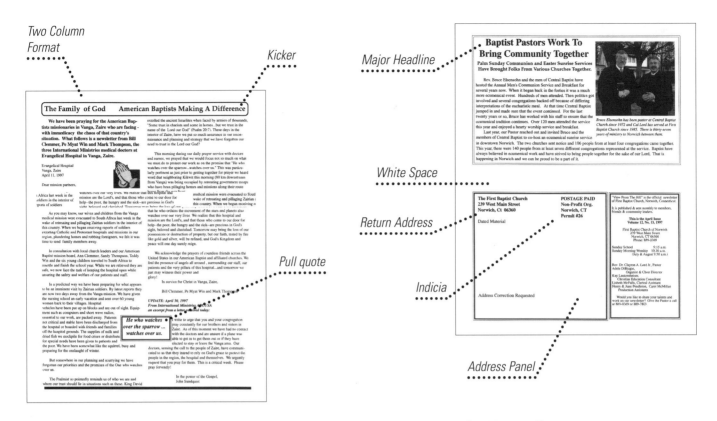

Using a logo or an illustration in the nameplate taps into the imagination of the reader. Notice that "The Lamplighter" and "The Planter" catch the eye.

The Nameplate

Several elements of a newsletter appear in each issue. The first is the nameplate (sometimes called the banner or the flag).

The nameplate identifies the newsletter as an official publication of the church and tells the reader who is sending it. Be creative when designing the nameplate. Think up a thought-provoking name for the newsletter and design the nameplate around it. Use the nameplate to make a statement about the church's ministry.

Since the nameplate is a repeating element in the newsletter, it needs to be easily recognizable. The basic elements of a nameplate include the name of the newsletter and the church, the date of publication, and issue number. Some churches add logos or illustrations to complement their names. This is great. Many churches use pictures of their church buildings. This is not necessarily the most effective nameplate design. Most newsletter readers know what the church looks like. It is better for the nameplate to describe the church's ministry.

The Calendar

A weekly or monthly calendar allows the reader to scan for useful information without having to navigate a sea of information. It is probably the most useful part of the newsletter because it contains all church activities in a nutshell. Many people tear out the calendar and save it or copy pertinent information to their personal planners. There are many calendar formats. Some include lists and schedules. The calendars shown on the right suggest a few different formats.

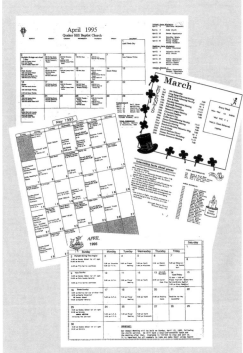

Calendars can be used to share information that readers need to know. Some churches use them to note birthdays and anniversaries as well as scheduled church events.

If the calendar appears too crowded, people will tend to skip over it. A good church calendar is one that the reader will look at and use.

Leave plenty of space for the reader to jot down personal obligations on the calendar, and it may be the one that ends up on the bulletin board or refrigerator.

The Masthead

The masthead is a third repeating element in a newsletter. It includes publication information such as staff members' names, the church's address, and phone numbers. A few examples of typical mastheads appear above.

The Mailing Space

If the newsletter is mailed, a space on the back cover has to be set aside for mailing information. Postal regulations suggest that the space be at least three inches tall and five inches wide. The indicia, or nonprofit mailing information, should be in the upper right-hand corner of the space, and there should be room for an address or a mailing label in the center.

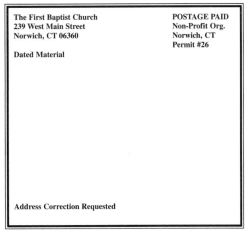

The Front Page

Newspaper editors have long recognized that the front page is what captures the reader's attention or loses it. Every edition of your newsletter offers the same challenge. The front page should present the most important or exciting news of your ministry.

Too many church newsletters put a letter from the pastor on the front page and bury the important news people want to read inside. Use the front page to tell about the Sunday school party or the senior adult trip to the Christian center. Use the front page to announce the upcoming CROP walk or special anniversary worship service. A well-designed front page entices the casual reader to look at the rest of the newsletter. Use the front page to tell your good news!

The Paper: Size, Setup, and Color

The size of the page and the color of the paper one chooses constitute a major aspect of the newsletter's appearance.

Size and Setup

The choice of page size is limited by the duplication equipment used and the money available.

- The standard newsletter is printed on 8 1/2 x 11-inch paper. The pages are usually held together by a staple in the left corner, but this format might be awkward to handle.

- The book, or bulletin, format, which uses letter-sized paper turned sideways, gives the reader two side-by-side 5 1/2 x 8-inch pages. The pages are stapled together in the middle with a saddle stapler.

- Using legal-sized paper produces a newsletter with slightly larger pages, 8 1/2 x 14 inches or 7 x 8 inches.

- Some copy machines can accommodate 11 x 17-inch ledger paper. This produces a magazine-style newsletter. When folded in the middle, the ledger-sized paper gives two letter-sized pages. This paper size eliminates the corner stapling problem mentioned earlier, and the centerfold can support several columns of print. The pages are large enough to provide an attractive appearance but small enough to be handled conveniently.

- Tabloid-sized pages need to be done by a professional printer. They can be up to seventeen inches long. These read like newspapers and are the largest size recommended.

Color

Black ink and white paper make a newsletter that is easy to read. Colored paper is a mixed blessing. The color makes the newsletter stand out, but once someone begins reading it, the color may interfere. Colored paper generally costs more too. If cost is a consideration, stick with white paper. If readability is a concern, go with white paper. Good design is the best way of making a newsletter stand out.

Organizing the Page

Effective layout organizes a page and helps guide the reader's eyes from one place to another. It helps the reader recognize what is of primary importance and what is secondary. Good organization arranges the two major elements of any page—the graphics (all the illustrations, photographs, lines, boxes, and borders) and the type (the lettering in the headlines and body of the article)—to create an attractive page appearance. Several tools help organize the page.

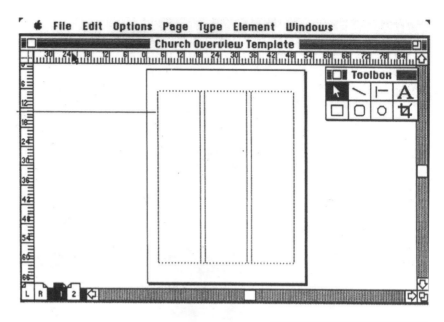

The Grid

A grid is a page-organizing tool that helps establish the overall structure of the page contents. It usually consists of horizontal and vertical lines that do not show when the page is copied. It serves as a guide for the placement of graphics and type and builds consistency from page to page or issue to issue. Grids also help in determining number of columns, margin size, headline placement, and more.

If you are using a typewriter, you place the grid under the page you are working on so that it defines the area where the graphics and type will fall. Many computer programs have built-in grids, like the one shown above, to aid in page design, and they are often set up with predetermined margins and column widths that can nevertheless be changed to suit personal preferences. The important thing about grids is that they help organize the page so that we can communicate our message more effectively.

Columns

Most pages are divided into two or more columns, which enhances the readability of the page. When more columns are used, each one becomes narrower and each line becomes shorter. Before you decide how many columns to use in your newsletter, consider that when we read, we

recognize groups of words as opposed to individual words. As the line gets shorter, the reader tends to read word by word, which slows down the process and discourages reading. It has been suggested that about six words per line is ideal. The width of the column also determines the size of the type. A wider column can be set in larger type, and a narrower column needs smaller type.

The size and placement of columns help to communicate our message. All columns do not have to be the same width. The grid can be set to produce a number of columns that enhances the message. If you are using a seven-column grid, for example, three columns can be used to support an illustration and the other four can form one wider column of text. Or if you are using a five-column grid, you can use one column for highlights and combine the remaining four columns into two columns of equal width. Each design produces a page with a different look.

This is what a typical grid looks like on the computer screen. The page is divided into columns in which you place the text. The dotted lines do not appear on the printed page.

Don't let the thought of designing a page scare you away from doing a newsletter. Use a grid to guide you in setting up columns, margins, and overall structure.

The left page of this spread was designed using a five-column format. Two of the columns were combined to give the page a different look. The right page has a simple two-column format. Together the columns form a nice contrast and add something exciting to the page. At the same time, the grid has allowed the designer to keep consistent margins and white space along the outside of the pages.

Margins, Alleys, and Gutters

Margins are also established with a grid. The margin is the white space surrounding the body of the text and graphics. The margin frames the page and helps ensure that the text is not cramped. Many of us try to include too much on a page. Adequate margins help avoid that problem. Type is dark, and too much of it can make a page look uninviting. The margins help brighten the appearance of the page, just as the space between the columns does. It is important to understand white space as the creative use of space, not the waste of it.

White space adds depth and proportion to a page. It places all the other elements in perspective as it helps organize the page and make sense of it.

White space that is used effectively has a distinctive shape that invites the reader into the written word.

The white space between two columns or two facing pages is called

The centerfold of this newsletter uses the space to give an overview of the whole year. The broad seven-column format and the use of white space, illustrations, and a large headline draws the reader in. The photograph in the center of the page highlights a significant event, and the graphics help direct the reader's attention across the page.

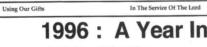

an alley, or a gutter. The space between two columns of related text should never be more than a quarter-inch wide, or the columns may seem disconnected from each other. The space between two columns of unrelated text can be wider, and the space between the two pages needs to be wide enough to accommodate whatever binds the pages. A creative approach regarding the centerfold of the document can make the two pages read like one large page. The newsletter editor can use the grids, columns, margins, and white space in any way that enhances the message.

Although the clip art breaks up the text above somewhat, the lack of white space makes this page look very dark. Wider margins and more white space between paragraphs would help lighten the page and make it more inviting.

Notice how the eye is drawn to the large photograph on the newsletter page to the left. It is no accident that it occupies the optical center of the page. Notice where the headline, the two photographs, and the text boxes are placed. They catch the eye and move it in a Z-pattern across the page, thus enabling the reader to perceive the important elements of the article.

Designing for the Roving Eye

Our eyes follow a pattern when we read, and it is helpful to be aware of this as we are laying out a page.

The Optical Center

The first thing to note is that the optical center of the page is three-eighths of the way down the page. Our eyes naturally fall on this place when we look at the page. It is just above the center of the page and slightly to the left or right. Some have speculated that this results from interpersonal eye contact. When two people talk to each other, one person's eyes are usually just above the other's field of vision. Each person's eyes search for the other's since eye contact is important. The newsletter designer must remember that this space is the ideal location for the most important message.

The Big Z

Just as the eye tends to find the center of the page, it also tends to keep moving across the page. The eye is in constant motion, and newsletter designers can take advantage of this. The eye typically begins scanning a page at the optical center and then moves to the lower left and back across the page to the lower right corner in a Z-shaped pattern. This is a good thing to remember as we design. We can set up our page to capture our reader's attention at every point.

Calling Attention to the Message

There are other patterns that catch the eye as well. You can direct the reader's attention by including pictures that have subjects facing one way or the other. Text that is laid out in numerical sequence also helps direct the reader's attention. The eye tends to be initially attracted to larger illustrations and pictures and then moves to smaller ones. Those who study design call this the phenomenon of diminishing visual impact.

Balance: Creating Contrast but Maintaining Unity

The contrast between the text and the graphics or between the text and the white space on a page is important. It can put emphasis on the information that you want to communicate.

To achieve this contrast, each page of the newsletter needs to have a dominant piece. It can be a photograph, illustration, headline, or white space. This defines the page and makes it interesting to look at. A word of warning—avoid overloading a page with contrasting elements. Look at the newsletter on this page. The number of illustrations makes the page look confusing and produces a negative effect on the reader. One or two contrasting elements help break up the gray look of the page, but more suggest chaos.

The illustrations, photographs, headlines, and every other element that we use in laying out the page should work together to produce a sense of unity. Things on the page need to go together. Illustrations should emphasize what the text is saying. Each headline should reflect the character of the article it is announcing. Although we'll be talking about it later, all typefaces should be from the same family. You will know that you have found unity when each design element complements all others.

Too many contrasting elements on a page have a negative effect on the reader.

The eye tends to look for consistency on the printed page. The main difference between the professional and the amateur designer is that the former chooses from the many "tricks of the trade" to achieve a consistent look, while the amateur gives in to the urge to use all the fancy tools available. Just remember that you can say more by saying less, as long as the elements of a page are unified.

Conclusion

Good design is not simply a way to decorate a page. It is a way to capture your reader's attention and focus it on your message. A well-designed newsletter has:

- a nameplate that clearly identifies your church as the sender and stimulates the interest and curiosity of the reader,

- a front page that is attractive and says "READ ME" to the person who picks up the mail,

- paper that enhances the message and fulfills the mission of the newsletter,

- grids to arrange text and graphics so that they create a flow and invite the readers into the story,

- margins, alleys, and white space creatively used to give the newsletter a fresh look so that it will stand out from other mail,

- a calendar that is prominently placed and filled with useful information, and

- a sense of balance and unity that flows through the newsletter and gives the reader a sense of continuity.

Designing Articles That Will Be Read

Trying to Enter the Reader's World

Time is a precious commodity today. Recently *USA Today* ran a story featuring three average American families. The article made the point that most people feel pressed for time, and this affects what they choose to do.

Writers need to be aware that most people no longer sit down and read a newspaper or a newsletter all the way through. They skim through the pages quickly and look for anything that seems important. A typical reader looks at the headlines, photos, and illustrations to pick up as much information as possible while expending the least amount of time and energy.

An insightful newsletter editor can take advantage of this information by designing articles that recognize the reader's time constraints while communicating important news.

"Eye-Level" Writing

Researchers have studied how people respond to different forms of printed advertising and have come to some conclusions about how people process and act on what they read.

They found that 80 percent of readers could answer questions based on what was presented in headlines and subheads. Up to 60 percent of readers could answer questions about text that was in boxes or was illustrated with charts and graphs. But fewer than 10 percent of readers could tell them what was written in regular body copy. These tests confirm that people do not spend time reading every word in the paper. We should keep this information in mind as we design our newsletter articles.

Newsletter writing is more than just coming up with a story. It is fashioning headlines; it is laying out articles; it is presenting the facts in a clear and concise form. Look at the article shown on the next page. Most church newsletters include a letter from the pastor. It may be insightful and inspiring, but if it looks like this one, it may never be read. Does it look like a page from your newsletter?

Think about how you read the newspaper. Do you read it from cover to cover? Do you read every article? How do you decide what to read? Your answers to these questions will help you enter your reader's world.

The Pastor's Page

When I first thought of coming to serve the church back in 1985, I was not sure what the future would hold for this ministry. But I had two experiences that gave me a vision for what was ahead.

The first experience was a ride through the city with Paul Lorraine and Curt Brockway. They showed me the west side, the downtown area, Thamesville, East Great Plains, and Cherry Hill. All along the way they pointed out members' homes. Growing up in Colchester, I had always thought of Norwich as "the big city." But during that short ride I saw a different side of the city and tasted a bit of the pride and hope that its residents felt. And it was beckoning me to come.

The second experience was the view from the window in the pastor's office. When I arrived here, the new road in front of the church was nearing completion. There was a new bridge just below us as well as a four-lane blacktop road heading west. The marina was looking pretty good, and the renovated houses on Church Street had begun to give the city a lift. Looking out through that window suggested two things to me that day. First, that a new day was dawning for our city and our church. Even as I could see some of the changes taking place outside the window, I knew there would be changes on this side too. And that was a good sign. Second, this city was to be my new home and from that day forward I would be looking out that window with love.

When I searched for a name for our newsletter, "The View from the Hill" came to mind. I was immediately reminded of the hope that is ours because another looked down from a hill with love almost two thousand years ago and provided the reason for our coming together.

It has always been my hope that this newsletter would foster communication and would broaden our sense of Christian call, hope, and love. So may we come to reflect the love of God in Christ. As we move forward through our eighth year together, I pray that you will find "The View from the Hill" as uplifting and as inspiring as I have since those first days in the summer of '85.

Cal

What stands out on this page? What grabs the reader's attention? Not very much. With a little effort, this pastor's page can be turned into something that draws a reader in. By adding a headline, subheads, call outs, and graphics, we can make the same article much more appealing to the eye. Look at the article on the next page. At first glance it looks like something totally different. But it is not. It is essentially the same.

The three levels of information processing may be outlined as follows:

Level 1: Reading at a glance

- Headlines
- Subtitles
- Subheads
- Pull quotes or call outs
- Illustrations
- Photos

Eighty percent of readers remember what they see here.

View from Pastor's Window Offers Vision of Hope and Inspires Newsletter

I was not sure what we were getting into.

When I first thought of coming to serve the church back in 1985, I was not sure what the future would hold for this ministry. But I had two experiences that gave me a vision for what was ahead.

A ride across town

The first experience was a ride through the city with Paul Lorraine and Curt Brockway. They showed me the west side, the downtown area, Thamesville, East Great Plains, and Cherry Hill. All along the way they pointed out members' homes. Growing up in Colchester, I had always thought of Norwich as "the big city." But during that short ride I saw a different side of the city and tasted a bit of the pride and hope that its residents felt.

Looking out the window

The second experience was the view from the window in the pastor's office. When I arrived here, the new road in front of the church was nearing completion. There was a new bridge just below us as well as a four-lane blacktop road heading west. The marina was looking pretty good, and the renovated houses on Church Street had begun to give the city a lift.

The view from the hill was pretty good.

Looking out through that window suggested two things to me that day. First, that a new day was dawning for our city and our church. Even as I could see some of the changes taking place outside the window, I knew there would be changes on this side too. And that was a good sign. Second, this city was to be my new home and from that day forward I would be looking out that window with love.

What is in a name?

When I searched for a name for our newsletter, "The View from the Hill" came to mind. I was immediately reminded of the hope that is ours because another looked down from a hill with love almost two thousand years ago and provided the reason for our coming together.

It has always been my hope that this newsletter would foster communication and would broaden our sense of Christian call, hope, and love. So may we come to reflect the love of God in Christ as we worship and serve together on the hill.

Cal

> "I was not sure what the future held, but two things gave me a vision for what was ahead."

> "And from that day forward I'd be looking out that window with love."

Level 2: Looking a Little Deeper

- Short articles
- Stories or data boxed off separately from body copy
- Graphs, tables, and diagrams
- Sidebars

Up to 60 percent of the readers will remember what they see in boxes or charts and graphs.

Level 3: Reading the Whole Package

- The body of news copy

Only 10 percent of readers will read every word. The percentage increases among people who are waiting for your newsletter to arrive.

Headlines: Level-One Writing

Headers are not headlines.

Many church newsletters use headers (or column headings) to outline the various sections of the paper. The headers label each section but contain little content. The pastor's page we looked at on page 28 provides a good example of this. The text is categorized by a particular person, group, or event. This may organize the material, but it does little to draw the reader in. Consider the following headers:

Pastor's Column

Choir Notes

Board Minutes

Youth News

Clearly, readers have a better chance of remembering information included in levels 1 and 2.

These are all examples of headers, or column headings. They help organize a page but do little to invite the busy reader in.

Headlines are better because they reveal the heart of a story in a few words.

Headlines tell a story. They outline an action. They inspire and invite. Which of the two headlines below stimulates your interest?

Persistent young man interrupts service to ask, "Who is Jesus?"

Or

Youth leader helps with "Children's Moment"

Both of these headlines could lead into the same story. The first one paints a picture in the reader's mind before she reads the story. The second one is matter of fact. It tells something that happened, but it may or may not capture the reader's interest.

The example below combines headers and headlines. The article is framed by the header "Sunday School Notes," but the headline invites the reader to go deeper.

Sunday School Notes

Senior adult class celebrates Passover seder with preschoolers

Here are a few tips for using headlines.

- **Always use a verb.**
  Verbs stress action and draw the reader in. They bring a story to life. Any headline can be rewritten to include a verb (action word).

- **Use longer headlines.**
  If 80 percent of your newsletter audience read only the headlines, it makes sense to include more useful information in them. Do not be afraid to use a two- or three-deck headline to summarize the story and share information.

- **Use headlines to reflect the central idea.**
  The headline should summarize the important aspects of the story. Try rewriting your lead sentence in headline fashion, and you should have a winner.

- **Strive for clarity.**
  Be specific. Try to write as clearly as possible. Avoid confusing phrases. Do not break up a headline in a way that misleads the reader.

- **Be positive.**
  Strive to come up with headlines that offer positive and upbeat information rather than negative statements about persons or events.

- **Follow standard capitalization rules.**
  Standard capitalization rules for titles and headlines according to *The Chicago Manual of Style,* 14th edition, are as follows: Capitalize first and last words and all nouns, pronouns, adjectives, verbs, adverbs, and subordinating conjunctions (if, because, as, that, etc.). Do not capitalize articles (a, an, the), coordinating conjunctions (and, but, or, for, nor), or prepositions, unless they are the first or last words of the title or headline, and do not capitalize the *to* in infinitives.

  You may choose to follow this style, which is used by most publishers.

Another style that is being used in some publications is to capitalize only the first word of the headline and lowercase all other words. Capitalizing every letter in every word is an unacceptable style since this makes the headline harder to read.

Initial Caps

Softball Team Wins a "Nail Biter" in Overtime

Down Style

Softball team wins a "nail biter" in overtime

All-Church Celebration Will Mark Adele's 15 Years as Organist

It All Began Fifteen Years Ago

Fifteen years ago Adele DiBiagio began as our part-time, temporary, fill-in organist and choir director. We didn't know where things would lead, but after all this time, we are very glad that the music committee decided to ask her to stay on to serve us. She has been wonderful, always working diligently to provide inspirational and challenging musical leadership.

Adele Has Played for Our SUNL Association and Our State Convention

She has served as organist and musical director for choral events in Norwich, for our SUNL Baptist Association and even for the ABCCONN state convention. And she has done it without ever being coerced!

We Are Going to Honor Adele

In recognition of this landmark anniversary, we are going to take up an offering so that we can give her a vacation package as a token of our appreciation. Our goal for this offering is $300.

Here's How You Can Show Your Appreciation

If you would like to help, please give your gift to Cynthia Strouse, Lori Lord, or Rosie Main. Or you can mail it to the church office with attention to the music committee. Checks can be made payable to the First Baptist Church. Just make sure you designate the gift for Adele's anniversary.

Using Subheads to Break Up the Text

Subheads are used to break up long sections of text and make them more readable. The subheads in the article above function as headlines in that they capture the central idea of each following paragraph. They help the reader get a sense of what the whole article is about before reading it.

Using Call Outs

The call out is a quote pulled out from the article that is set off and enlarged, usually within two clearly defined lines or a box. It attracts the reader's attention and invites further reading. Call outs can also be called blurbs, breakouts, or pull quotes. The revamped pastor's page provides an example of how they are used. Look at any magazine and you will find several call outs. As a newsletter writer, you can use them any time you have a long article. Call outs lift up important points, break up the text, and make the whole page more attractive.

One word of caution is appropriate. Don't cramp the call out into a small space. It will frustrate your efforts to get your point across. These boxes both say the same thing, but a message that is cramped looks too busy and turns readers off.

> "I just told them I realized how much God loves me."

> "I just told them I realized how much God loves me."

Give yourself enough room to make the message really stand out to the reader.

One last point needs to be made. Call outs can also be enclosed in boxes that cut across the columns, or they can be placed within the columns and set apart in a larger print and separated with lines as shown here.

God Gives Us All We Need to Get Work Done

Many people assume that if God wants to do something or get something done, God just does it. A careful look at Scripture, however, reveals that God very rarely does anything alone. When God wants to bring something to pass on earth, his normal method of operation is to use believing people. These people are you and I, the Church.

Often people shut God out of their business dealings and financial lives.

One illustration of this truth is found in Deuteronomy 8:18, "But thou shalt remember the Lord thy God: for it is He that giveth thee power to get wealth, that He may establish His Covenant."

Often people shut God out of their business dealings and financial lives, believing that this area of life is simply up to them. But our Scripture verse says we are to remember the Lord. He is to be an integral part of our financial lives.

We should pray over our businesses and jobs. We should study God's Word, seeking divine wisdom about these things. Excluding God from our finances is foolishness on our part, "for it is He that giveth thee power to get wealth."

God has given to you the ability to make money. Have you ever thought about that? The money you need and that God wants you to have in this life will not be "rained down from heaven."

God can provide in miraculous ways, but most often this provision comes as we exercise the ability he has given us to make money. We should ask ourselves the question God asked Moses, "What is that in thine hand?" God used something very common and ordinary, a rod, to do some very uncommon and extraordinary things.

There are abilities God has put "in thine hand"—your hand—that may seem very common and ordinary. But they can be turned into money with the help and direction of the Lord.

Why does God give you the power to gain wealth? "That God may establish his covenant," says the Bible. God wants to advance the cause of Christ on earth. God wants his kingdom to grow and increase. Yes, God could do it alone, but that's simply not his way. God wants you.

God's normal method of operation is to use us to do his will.

One of the ways God establishes his covenant is by blessing our church through your financial gifts. By blessing our church, God is able to bless the lives of people through us because we are the Church.

By joining hearts and hands along with the combined efforts of our God-given abilities to make money, we're able to advance the work of the Church and establish God's covenant here on earth.

Bite-Sized Chunks of Information: Level-Two Writing

If all stories could be told in a single paragraph, more people would read them. The average reader wants to get in and out of a story. The newsletter below capitalizes on level-two writing.

Notice that each article is brief and to the point. Each is no more than three paragraphs long. Most are illustrated with a graphic.

The reader can scan the page quickly but come away with a lot of information.

Level-two writing includes three characteristics that capture the reader's attention:

- *Short sections of body copy.* Tell the story in a paragraph or two and then move on. Use subheads to

A chart, graph, or diagram can usually speak for itself. USA Today has become famous for its use of graphs to depict trends in American society.

THE VIEW FROM THE HILL

The First Baptist Church of Norwich
ISSUE 1, VOLUME 8, JULY 1992

Rev. Clayton A. Lord Jr., Pastor
Phone: 889-0369 (Church)
              889-7803 (Home)

Summer Sunday Morning Worship   9:30 a.m.

239 West Main Street, Norwich, CT 06360
affiliated with the American Baptist Churches U.S.A.

We Are Trying A New Look For Our Newsletter!

A little education is a very dangerous thing. The Pastor attended a newsletter seminar last week and he came back with all kinds of "crazy ideas." He went as a part of his continuing research into intra-church communication as part of his doctoral thesis. This new format is just one of the things that he came back with. Each page of the newsletter will have a particular focus, such as; "coming events", "people news" "what's happening", "fun and inspiration" and should be a little more readable. Let me know what you think!

Worship Hour Moves To Earlier Time For July and August .

As summer heats up, we will be moving our morning worship ahead one hour. From July 5 through Labor Day we will be meeting at 9:30 a.m.

Part of the reason for this move is simply due to the climate. The sanctuary becomes extremely warm in the summer months and in order to enjoy the serenity and worshipful atmosphere that it offers, we can try to beat some of the heat by meeting earlier.

A second reason is the simple fact that we believe that worship is important all year round. Therefore, we want to offer our summer vacationers a challenge. If they come to worship we'll give them an earlier, inspirational, start to their day.

Summer Sermons

In July, we will draw our exploration of Paul's Epistles to a close with four sermons that will help us move forward in faith.

On July 5th, at the 9:30 a.m. hour, we'll look at the letter to the *Galatians* in a sermon titled, **"Getting to the Bottom Line!"** We will also celebrate the Lord's supper during the service.

On July 12th, we'll explore the letters to the Thessalonians with the message, **"Getting To The Punch Line!"**

Baptists Plan Trip to See the Red Sox Invade the Yankees in the Bronx...

Plans are being made for a group to go to Yankee Stadium on Saturday, August 8th to see the visiting *Red Sox* take on the *Bronx Bombers*. The group will plan to meet at the church and travel down together. We will be ordering tickets on Monday, July 6th. If you would like to go, please speak to the Pastor. The cost is about $7.00 a piece

"Getting To The Hidden Treasure", will be the message when we gather on July 19th as we look at II Corinthians.

Finally, we will finish the series by looking at Paul's epistle to Titus. The sermon will be **"Getting To The Golden Rule"** on July 26th.

So join us for worship each week this month!

break up a longer story and keep the reader's interest. Separate paragraphs with a line to add white space and give the story a brighter, lighter appearance. Mystery writer Elmore Leonard says, "I try to leave out the parts that people skip."

- *Text boxes.* The eyes gravitate toward anything that is set off. Use boxes for your most important messages. A lot of editors include lists, tips, schedules, and important announcements in boxes. This highlights the information and adds an interesting design element.
- *Graphs, charts, diagrams, and other illustrations.* These elements can be used to communicate important information and statistics. They can be used to illustrate and thus emphasize almost anything. The illustration and its caption can define the message more succinctly than a whole page of text.

Getting the Point Across: Level-Three Writing

Level-three writing is what we use to tell the stories that we want people to hear. The first two writing levels are used to capture a reader's attention. Our effectiveness on this third level will determine whether or not we communicate our message.

It has been suggested that the average person is subjected to over fifteen hundred commercial images a day. Newspapers, magazines, and books call out to potential readers with their messages. Radio stations and television networks broadcast their messages like buckshot across the nation, hoping for profitable connections. At the end of the day, the average person is not interested in reading long sections of bland body copy. Those who hope to win readers' attention must tell their stories imaginatively and succinctly.

Here are six tips for good level-three writing:

- Get to the point
- Get personal
- Tell one story at a time
- Present timely messages
- Accentuate the positive
- Write for the reader's eye

Get to the Point

Cut right to the chase. It is not necessary to include detailed background information or personal histories for every story you write. Say what needs to be said and move on. When you choose to include a story, do not make excuses for doing so. The story should speak for itself. Think of your writing as an ongoing dialogue with the reader from month to month or week to week. Do not include endless repetitions of common knowledge.

Get Personal

Tell stories about real people and mention them by name. This adds appeal to the articles. It brings them to life and helps the reader connect with the action. Most people like to be recognized, and most like to read what is written about their friends and neighbors.

Tell One Story at a Time

A major story covering several paragraphs may be too much for a reader to work through all at once. Writing several small stories that deal with a single event is a much more effective way to get a message across. The reader can swallow information more easily when it is in bite-sized chunks.

Present Timely Messages

People read and remember messages that are important. A message that is about something still in the future is apt to be overlooked and forgotten long before the event occurs. A

Jesus used parables and anecdotes to help his audience form pictures in their minds of what he was saying. We can take a lesson from our Master.

message that recalls some event that happened several months ago may be skipped right over. When writing for level three, concentrate on timely matters. Give the details of events that are happening in the near future or record the events of something that has just occurred. Point out dates and times and help the reader sense the immediacy. Level-two writing is better suited for pointing out future calendar dates.

Accentuate the Positive

Church newsletters should bear glad tidings. Try to accentuate the positive in every article. The way of the world is to focus on the negative. Your readers probably get enough of that every day. If you share good news, they will actually look forward to reading your articles.

Write for the Reader's Eye

Write stories that help the reader develop a picture of what is being described. Use metaphors and word pictures to illustrate what you are talking about. Jesus did this well when he used parables to tell his stories about eternal truths. People not only heard what he was saying but also pictured it in their minds.

Conclusion

There are three levels of writing that can be used to put across a message to readers. Use all three to communicate effectively.

Level 1
- Headlines
- Subtitles
- Subheads
- Call outs
- Photos and illustrations

Level 2
- Short articles
- Boxed and bulleted information
- Sidebars
- Graphs, diagrams, and captions

Level 3
- Body copy

Effective Writing for the Newsletter

Writing with a Purpose

Good layout attracts the reader's attention, but design is only the first step in the process of putting together a great newsletter. After form comes content. This is where effective writing is essential.

Writing for a church newsletter is a labor of love. Many people find writing difficult, but it is something that anyone can learn to do who is willing to take enough time to develop a few basic skills.

Writing must be done with a purpose in mind, especially when it comes to church newsletters. Earlier we noted that the mission of the church and the goals of the newsletter must be stated before beginning a newsletter. The same principle holds true for writing individual newsletter articles.

Most articles will be written to inform, invite, or inspire the readers. The purpose of an article shapes what is written.

Writing to Invite

If the intent of an article is to invite the reader to participate, the writing should be infused with an air of expectancy and excitement that motivates the reader to act on the invitation.

Writing to Inform

Articles that are meant to inform should be factual but also personal. They should include the who, the where, and the why. These stories should be written to give the reader a mental image of what is being said. Do not give just "the facts." Share what they mean as well. *USA Today* uses graphs, pictures, and short stories to explain everyday statistics and what they mean. As a result, most of these information clips can stand independently.

Writing to Inspire

Stories that are written to inspire others need to have identifiable characters. The reader needs to feel a connection with the subject of this type of story. Stories that inspire touch deep chords in readers because they create images of vision and hope.

Writing is putting a thought on paper and then shaping it into a coherent sentence.

37

Reporting the Facts

Knowing what you want to do is the first step. A second step is relaying the facts to the reader. Everyone has heard of the "five Ws" of effective writing: who, what, when, where, and why. If you are really on the ball, you can add "how" to the list too. Good newsletter writing begins by answering all the questions that readers will have. List all of the facts before you even begin to write a paragraph.

Professional journalists use a format called the "inverted pyramid" to shape the facts into a story. The most important facts are always listed first. Anything else that needs to be shared is then written in order of importance. The least important aspects of the story are saved for the end.

Once we have the facts, our writing should start with a minisummary of the entire article in the first sentence. Newspaper reporters call this the "lead sentence." A good lead sentence provides essential information and draws the reader into the story. Many readers look at the first sentence or two of a story and then decide whether or not they will read the whole story. Thus we need to give the essence of the story up front to get our news to the widest audience.

Composing a good lead sentence takes time and patience. Some writers suggest writing the first sentence last. After you write the article, go back over the story and pull out the most important or most exciting element and turn it into your lead. This will captivate the audience and draw readers into the story.

The first draft of any article is never the last. The five Ws provide the writer with a framework, but the work of writing takes place as an article is written and rewritten. The first draft allows the writer to get his or her thoughts on paper, where they can be molded and shaped. The second, third, and subsequent drafts will sharpen the focus of what is written and help clarify meaning.

Writing on a word processor or a computer takes a lot of the pain out of the writing process. Words and phrases can be changed and modified without a great deal of added work. Today there is no excuse for not rewriting and reworking the first drafts of the newsletter.

A good technique for testing what you have written is to read the article back to yourself and ask if it says what you mean it to say. Will the readers understand your message, or will they get bogged down by the words and phraseology? If so, it is time to do another rewrite.

Seven Tips for News Writers

Brevity and clarity are key elements in the third step of newsletter writing. It is not necessary to write voluminously when reporting church news. Here are seven tips for writing good newsletter stories.

Use little words and short sentences.

We live in the era of the "sound bite." People want facts presented clearly for quick scanning. Many readers want simple words that are direct and to the point. Do not use the newsletter to show your vast vocabulary; it will only discourage the reader from looking at your writing. You can use single-syllable words to convey your meaning clearly.

Simple, short sentences also help readability. Avoid run-on sentences. Long, complicated sentences can be divided into shorter ones. If a sentence has more than twenty words, the reader is apt to lose interest.

Short paragraphs are also more apt to draw readers in. Make the point and then stop or start a new paragraph.

Paint word pictures.

Stimulate the reader's interest by using metaphors and images that engage the

Try using short words. They hasten the pace of reading, move the reader along, and help develop narrative flow.

senses. Help readers to see, hear, feel, or smell what you are talking about, and you will have them reading the entire story.

Avoid cold, technical language unless it is central to the story. It tends to put distance between you and the reader. Use a metaphor to relay information if possible.

Use the active voice.

Sentences that are expressed in the active voice are more vivid and thus more interesting. For example, the verb in the sentence, "Mary took the money to the bank," is in the active voice. Mary is acting. She is taking the money. Many writers think that the passive voice sounds more objective, but usually it just sounds more vague—for example, "The money was taken to the bank." This sentence slows the reader down by forcing her to think about who is doing what, when it is never actually stated. Watch out for "to be" verbs. An alarm should go off in your head when you see phrases like "was taken" because you are entering the "Passive Zone."

Use clear nouns and strong verbs to communicate your message.

Do not try to spice up your story with a lot of adjectives and adverbs. The most readable stories are the ones that say it simply. For example, which of these two sentences is easier to read?

Mary erupted with emotion after the performance.

Mary was moved by her intense emotions after the great performance.

The first sentence is more intense and relays a stronger sense of action. Notice that fewer words are used as well.

Edit out all unnecessary words.

It is very easy to use more words than you need. Check for words that are overused and try to replace them for variety.

Resist putting yourself in the story. Phrases like "I think" and "I believe" only detract from your credibility. They also create a barrier between you and the reader. Edit yourself out of the story.

Cutting out unnecessary words can shorten a newsletter article dramatically. Many long, wordy announcements can be cut in half.

For example, there are fifty-four words in the following paragraph. It can be shortened by deleting unnecessary words.

George Rezendes, our moderator, has called for a special church meeting to adopt the proposed by-laws for Sunday, December 11, following our morning worship service. He hopes that everyone who can be there will make an attempt to be there. If approved, the new by-laws would shape the church organization for 1995 and after.

Dropping the nonessential words leaves:

Moderator George Rezendes has called a special meeting after the morning worship on Sunday, December 11, to adopt the proposed by-laws. He hopes everyone will try to be there. If approved, the new by-laws will shape the church organization for 1995 and after.

By applying some principles already mentioned, we can cut still more words.

Please stay for the meeting following worship on December 11 to vote on proposed by-laws that will shape our church in the future.

By making a few simple changes, we came up with a concise, easy-to-read paragraph. All editing does not have to be so dramatic, but with a little practice,

---

Use the active voice!

Try writing:

John went to Disney World on vacation.

instead of:

A vacation to Disney World was taken by John.

Or write:

Susan hit the robber with her pocketbook.

instead of:

The pocketbook was used by Susan to hit the robber.

we can develop a capacity for concise expression.

Say what you mean.

Avoid clichés, cute phrases, and insider language. Clichés are tiresome and discourage the reader. Cute phrases are little more than fluff that inflates a story needlessly while obscuring the message. Insider language creates a barrier for those who do not know the organizational in and outs. The goal of producing a newsletter is to inform your readers. These phrases tend to exclude and thus alienate people.

Just be straightforward and honest. Tell it like it is. Report what you know, and the readers will respect you for that. Church newsletters generally enjoy a high level of readership. Ninety percent of those who receive a newsletter read some part of it. But if you ever betray your readers' trust, they will not bother to read what you write.

The newsletter is not a pulpit from which to preach at people. Hurling guilt or condemnation at readers will lose them. People read by choice. If your work is associated with "bad news," it will lose its welcome in the homes where it is sent.

Proofread your work.

Check spelling, grammar, and punctuation in each story. It is common to read through an article and find that a letter, a word, or a punctuation mark is missing. This is especially true when revisions are done on the video monitor of a word processor or computer. Our eyes tend to gloss over a lot of the text.

Reading is done without the benefit of prosodic cues, which help a person determine the meaning of a given communication. Timing, stress, pitch, and vocal intonation help the hearer understand a spoken message. In writing, punctuation and grammatical position of words accomplish this. Because the writer is not there to

Good writing comes out of rewriting. Write it. Then write it again. Get rid of any unnecessary words and phrases in each successive edition and keep paring the story down until it hits the mark. Aim for brevity and clarity.

explain what he or she means, the text has to speak for itself. It is always a good idea to have a dictionary handy, to run the spell checker on the computer, or to have a proofreader available on the newsletter staff.

Conclusion

Legend has it that William Shakespeare wrote his greatest works without ever erasing a line. Words just came to him and he wrote them down. For most writers, however, writing is a deliberate process of bringing words together in sentences to tell someone a story.

A writer needs to determine who the audience is and what purpose the writing will serve before penning the first word. Writers need to ask the following questions:

1. Who is the reader?
2. Do I want to inform, invite, or inspire the reader?
3. What are the facts? Name the five Ws.
4. How will I lead into the story?

Once you have answered these questions, you are ready to begin writing. After you have written the first draft, be sure to revise and rewrite for clarity.

Keys to Effective Writing

Know your audience.

- Include specific information readers want.
- Write with a specific response in mind.
- Express your care, concern, and support for what your readers are doing.
- Answer the question, "So what?" for the reader.

Begin by giving the facts.

- In the first paragraph concentrate on the five Ws: who, what, where, when, why [and how].
- Find the most important element and put it in the lead sentence.

Check your information for accuracy.

- Check dates and times.
- Spell names correctly.

Be simple and straightforward.

- Say what you mean. Make it short and sweet.
- Use short sentences and simple words.
- Avoid big words or lots of modifiers.

Rewrite, rewrite, rewrite.

- Get it down on paper even if it isn't perfect the first time.
- Look at it and then improve it.

Edit out all cute and trite phrases.

- Use metaphors.

Use the active voice.

- Have the subject perform the action.

Use action verbs.

- Keep your stories moving.
- Make your stories exciting.
- Use words that help readers visualize action.

Using Type in the Newsletter

7

Designing a Page with Type

Gutenberg's marvelous invention in 1440—the printing press—revolutionized the Western world by making the printed word available to the common person. For the first time in history, books could be printed and distributed in large quantities. The laborious, time-consuming effort of copying manuscripts by hand would soon be a thing of the past. The quality of a page printed on a press was impressive, surpassing anything of that day.

It is no exaggeration to assert that similarly, the introduction of the personal computer and numerous desktop publishing programs has changed the world of newsletter production. Not too long ago, the biggest decision the editor had to make was what news went into the newsletter. Today the editor can control every element of newsletter design from layout to typeface. Each decision colors the look of the publication.

Today's publisher can use the computer to design a newsletter from A to Z. We have already discussed design and layout. Now it is time to talk about the two graphic elements used in newsletter design: the illustrations and the type. Illustrations are the pictures, cartoons, drawings, graphs, charts, and photographs that are used to support the text. These illustrations will be discussed more fully in chapters 9 and 10.

Typeface or font is the style of type that gives the text a special look. Type is created in hundreds of different styles that have unique characteristics. The differing characteristics make each style of type suitable for particular uses. The use of type and its deliberate placement on the page, whether in body copy or in headlines, has become more prominent since people began using computers to compose and produce their newsletters. The desktop explosion has enabled millions of people to "set type." This development occurred because most computers come loaded with a variety of typefaces from which to choose.

The introduction of the personal computer has changed the world of newsletter production. Today the editor can control every element of newsletter design from layout to typeface.

The Architecture of Type

Typeface

The typeface is the actual letter we see printed on the page. Much of the terminology associated with type goes back to the first days of the printing press. In the days of Gutenberg all type was set by hand for the presses. Each piece of type was set on metal and was called a "stamp." The terms used in Gutenberg's day to describe type are still used today.

The typeface is what you see on the page. It is called the "face" because in the first presses it was the part of the stamp that was raised and touched the page. Every typeface has a distinct personality that will affect the look and feel of the publication in which it is used.

Typestyle

The design of some basic styles of type had to do with aspects of the culture that existed at the time. For example, black-letter typeface was typical of the European handwriting of Gutenberg's day; Old English is an example of this style. It is also referred to as black-letter type because of its heavy presence. It is one of the hardest types to read and is not popular today.

> **𝔒𝔩𝔡 𝔈𝔫𝔤𝔩𝔦𝔰𝔥 𝔥𝔞𝔰 𝔞 𝔥𝔢𝔞𝔳𝔶, 𝔡𝔞𝔯𝔨 𝔞𝔭𝔭𝔢𝔞𝔯𝔞𝔫𝔠𝔢. 𝔍𝔱 𝔴𝔞𝔰 𝔬𝔫𝔢 𝔬𝔣 𝔱𝔥𝔢 𝔢𝔞𝔯𝔩𝔦𝔢𝔰𝔱 𝔱𝔶𝔭𝔢𝔣𝔞𝔠𝔢𝔰.**

Old-style typefaces are characterized by bracket-style serifs and long vertical strokes. The serifs are the horizontal "feet" at the end of the vertical strokes of each letter. Serif typefaces are easier to read, since the serifs visually connect the letters and help the reader's eye move along the lines. The serifs actually help the reader see the type as

---

Here is just a small selection of some of the typefaces available for personal computers. Although each face shown is the same point size, the visual size of the letters appears different.

Bernhard Fashion   ThOR   Times

Architectura   Marigold   NEULAND

Colossalis   Onyx   Helvetica

Eras   Koch Antiqua   Giddyup

CHARLEMAGNE   Dom Casual

Present Script   Bodoni   Choco

The x-height is the size of the letter x or an average lowercase letter.

The cap line is the line that runs across all the capitals. In some faces the ascenders rise above the cap line.

Ascenders are the parts of the letters that rise above the x-height.

Designing with Type

Descenders are the parts of the letters that go below the baseline.

The serifs are the small 'feet' at the end of vertical strokes.

The point size is the height of the capitals and descenders plus enough leading not to touch the ascenders of the following line.

words rather than letters. The serifs also add character and flair. Times, Bookman, and Palatino are favorite typefaces.

The tiny serifs help make Times Roman easy to read.

Square serif type is great for posters and circus flyers. The sample below demonstrates how the type stands out and calls for us to read it. It has come to be associated with the old west.

Serif and sans serif

Sans serif simply means "without serif." The sans serif typefaces such as Helvetica (or Arial) are good for headlines. They are simple and functional, but they are not good to use for text in long articles. They make reading more difficult because the eye has a harder time distinguishing between letters.

WANTED: Dead or Alive

Helvetica has a very clean, crisp appearance on the page. However, it is difficult to read a long paragraph printed in this face because it has no serifs. The eye gets tired because it has to stop at every letter to identify it.

On the other hand,

Helvetica Looks Great in Headlines.

Script typefaces are used for fancy printing on invitations and awards. They imitate handwriting or

You are invited to use Snell Roundhead on your next invitation.

calligraphy and are great for special effects produced on the computer.

Here are some examples of "special" typefaces. Note their differences.

Spumoni

ABCDEFGHIJKLMNOPQRSTUVWXYZ

Symbol

ΑΒΧΔΕΦΓΗΙϑΚΛΜΝΟΠΘΡΣΤΥςΩΞΨΖ

Zapf Dingbats

Finally, some typefaces are referred to as "special." Symbol gives us the Greek alphabet. Dingbats are typographical symbols that are commonly used as ornaments.

Families of Type

Families of type have names that were derived from various sources. Some are named after their designers, such as Zapf and Bodoni. Others get their names from their original uses. Times Roman, for example, was designed in the early part of the twentieth century for the *London Times*. Century was first used on the pages of *Century* magazine. Berkeley was first designed for the University of California at Berkeley. The history of type can be as interesting as the faces themselves.

Each family includes a number of variations of type within that typeface. For example, light or book, bold, semibold and heavy or black, plus the italics and condensed versions for these weights are common variations within a family. They can be used effectively both to vary and to complement each other on the printed page. Be warned, though, that outline and shadow are not really designs, but are computer enhancements that may not reproduce well.

Type Size and Weight

The typeface that you choose for your newsletter exerts a major impact on its appearance. Each has its own distinctive characteristics, whether short and fat or tall and skinny.

The weight of the type is determined by the width, or thickness, of the strokes of the letters. Some letters appear to be much heavier than others.

Type is measured in points. When we choose a typeface, we need to choose a point size as well. The points are part of a system of measurement. There are twelve points to a pica and six picas to an inch. Measuring type can be misleading because the point system actually measures the space *around* the letter, not the letter itself. As a result, two typefaces with the same point size can be very different in actual size. Look at the example following for an illustration of this.

B   *B*

New York   Choco

Both are 36 points in size.

Meet the Univers Family

Univers 45 Light
Univers 45 Light Oblique
Univers 47 Light Condensed
Univers 47 Light Condensed Oblique
Univers 55 Regular
Univers 55 Oblique
Univers 57 Condensed
Univers 57 Condensed Oblique
Univers 65 Bold
Univers 65 Bold Oblique
Univers 67 Bold Condensed
Univers 67 Bold Condensed Oblique
Univers 75 Black
Univers 75 Black Oblique

Each of the samples below is 30 points, but they look different. This is because each letter has a different x-height. The point size is based upon the x-height of that particular family. The difference in size is readily apparent. This is all due to the difference in x-height. Although each is set at 30 points, they appear to be different sizes.

Times   x Time waits for no one.

Helvetica   x Time waits for no one.

Chicago   xTime waits for no one.

Several elements are involved in determining the actual size of the letter. One of the factors is the height of the letter x, which is called the "x-height." The x-height changes from family to family. This measurement reflects the height of most lowercase letters.

Letters also have ascenders and descenders. These are the parts of the letters that go above or below the x-height. Some families have very short ascenders and descenders, causing the type to appear shorter. Others have long ascenders.

Long Neck
Short Neck

Thus the actual size of a letter in any family is determined by the point size, the x-height, the width, and the length of ascenders and descenders.

Using Space with Type

Space is an important element in page design. It can enhance the look and feel that readers experience when they open your newsletter. It can set a relaxed tone and help the reader's eyes move across the page. Effective use of white space can make your newsletter very reader friendly. All of this begins with the type.

The type you use, including all of the issues we have mentioned so far, will have a measurable effect on the white space the reader sees. The style of type determines how much space the letters take up on a line and how much white space appears on the rest of the page. When an editor does not understand how to use the space on the page effectively, the text can seem crowded, dark, and uninviting.

Type families with tall ascenders and descenders seem to bring the lines closer to each other. Conversely, shorter ascenders and descenders leave more space between lines.

The amount of white space determines the readability of the page. White space changes with the type, the leading, and the kerning. Leading is the space between lines. Kerning refers to the space between letters. Look at the text in the gray box on the following page. In the second example, the leading was increased to 2½ points above the point size. The paragraph is much easier to read, and the selection looks more open and inviting.

For the first two instances, 10 point Times Roman is used, for the third, 10 point New Aster. Each gives a different look to the same paragraph. They are on a line measure of the same width, but the New Aster runs longer because the letters are wider. In order to accommodate the whole paragraph in the New Aster typeface, we would need almost a third more space.

When using type:

- *Strive for a unified look.*

- *Give each type a specific role to play, that is, headlines, body, pull quotes, and so forth.*

- *Do not distract the reader by using multiple typefaces on the same page.*

Times Roman 10/10

The use of space is important when designing a page. Unfortunately, a lot of people take the space on the page for granted. The effective use of white space can make your newsletter very reader-friendly. The type you use and all of the things we have talked about so far will have a measurable effect on the white space the reader sees. As a matter of fact, the type we choose will determine how much space the letters will take up in a line and how much white space will appear on the rest of the page.

Times Roman 10/12.5

The use of space is important when designing a page. Unfortunately, a lot of people take the space on the page for granted. The effective use of white space can make your newsletter very reader-friendly. The type you use and all of the things we have talked about so far will have a measurable effect on the white space the reader sees. As a matter of fact, the type we choose will determine how much space the letters will take up in a line and how much white space will appear on the rest of the page.

New Aster 10/12.5

The use of space is important when designing a page. Unfortunately, a lot of people take the space on the page for granted. The effective use of white space can make your newsletter very reader-friendly. The type you use and all of the things we have talked about so far will have a measurable effect on the white space the reader sees. As a matter of fact, the type we choose will determine how much space the letters will take up in a line and how much white space will appear on the rest of the page.

Leading

The space between the lines is called leading (pronounced *ledding*). The name comes from the days when thin strips of lead were inserted between lines of type to make space. The amount of leading greatly affects the look of the page. Lines that are too close together give the document a dark, gray appearance and discourage the reader from looking at it.

The leading is the same between the first line of text and the headline as between the lines of text.

Who Needs More Rain?

With all of the rain water that has come down the mountainside, who needs more rain?

Five points of leading are added before the text to give the head breathing room while keeping it with the text.

Who Needs More Rain?

With all of the rainwater that has come down the mountainside, who needs more rain?

X-height and leading are two linked variables. In general, you can assume more leading will be needed as the x-height gets larger. Most typewriters are preset and cannot be modified. Most word processing applications have built-in initial (default) settings that automatically set the leading. But you can modify the leading to suit special needs.

An example of when it might be necessary to change the leading would be in setting headlines. Sometimes the type we choose will make them appear to be too far or too close to the body of the copy. We might adjust the leading so that the headline would appear more connected to the text.

Kerning

Kerning refers to adjusting the amount of space between two letters, which is sometimes necessary with larger type sizes or in lines set with full justification. Kerning can be useful in achieving a more graceful appearance by adjusting the space that exists between two letters, such as *AV* or *We*, which are almost always in headlines.

TRAVEL Travel

Unkerned

TRAVEL Travel

Kerned

If you are using left justification (all lines are even at the left margin, also called ragged right), there is usually no need to adjust the spacing between letters. However, if you are using full justification (lines at both left and right margins are even), more spacing problems will occur, particularly in lines with fewer characters.

For example, if we were using Palatino to type a story like this one, the reader's eyes would soon get tired if we didn't adjust the spacing a little bit.

This is much easier to read even though it is the same typeface as was used in the preceding paragraph.

Word-processing programs employ automatic kerning, and even though most of us will never bother to adjust it, it is good to know that it is there and how to use it. Consult your computer manual for details about how to adjust both the kerning and the leading.

Conclusion

Putting It All Together

The typeface you choose to use will give your publication a distinctive look. **Note:** Typefaces named after cities (Chicago, Geneva, Monaco, New York) were designed for use on the computer screen, not for typesetting and reproduction.

Helvetica has a larger x-height,

while Courier is known for its standard "typewriter" look, with each letter having the same amount of space, whether it is an *i* or a *w*.

If you decided to use Chicago type you would see that the letters are spaced a little wider apart in sans serif style and are a little bolder and heavier.

Choco gives a more frantic look and would be hard to read for very long. It is one of those special types we mentioned earlier.

New York is a serif type with loose spacing and a large x-height with normal ascenders and short descenders built into it,

as opposed to Times which is also a serif type, but very compact and crisp with tight spacing.

Geneva stands apart as being larger simply by virtue of a larger x-height for its sans serif characters.

All of the previous typefaces were set at 10 points, yet they are remarkably different in size and character. The choice of type alone can shape the look and appearance of your document. You can also choose to change the leading and kerning to customize your newsletter. Creative use of white space helps lighten the appearance of the page and makes it more inviting to the reader's eye.

Just remember...

- Maintain a sense of unity with the choice of type as you are working through the newsletter.
- Avoid the temptation to use too many typefaces (no more than three different faces on one page is the general rule, although many designers recommend using variations within one type family only).
- Strive to use a size and style of type that is suited for your audience and appropriate for your message.
- Use white space to bring out the type and the message it conveys.
- An effective use of type and space will help you deliver your message.

Molding and Shaping the Text

Shaping Text That Jumps Off the Page

After we write our stories, format our columns, and choose our typeface, we can begin to shape and mold the various design elements onto the page. To get started, we need to ask several questions.

- How will paragraphs be introduced?
- How will the type be aligned?
- Will graphics and illustrations be separate from the text or integrated into it?
- What kind of tabs will be used?
- Will special text be indented or set apart? If so, how?
- Will any special effects be used?

When it comes to producing a newsletter, there is more to writing than just the writing. In the next few pages we will examine these questions and look at the options available to us.

Column Width and Size

In chapter 4 we noted that column width and type size go hand in hand.

Long lines with small type are hard for the eye to follow. Short lines with large type tend to hinder the progress of reading. Some accommodation has to be made.

Researchers have found that the human eye looks for patterns and word groups as it scans a page of text. It makes a series of jumps across a line and passes information to the brain. These studies led one group of reading consultants to suggest that columns that consist of about six words per line are easiest to read. Thus the longer the line, the larger the type size should be to maintain this balance of words to column width.

Another group, emphasizing character recognition as opposed to word recognition, has suggested that the perfect column size can be determined by typing the alphabet one and a half times at the particular type size desired.

Clearly column width and type size are factors that determine readability. When you adjust one variable, you must also consider the other. Remember, the goal of putting out a newsletter is to pass on information to the reader. If you shape the text into

Does your text jump out at the reader? Does it break the surface of the page and call for the reader's attention?

With a few easy-to-learn tricks you can produce a newsletter filled with stories that jump off the page.

	6	12	18	24	30

abcdefghijklmnopqrstuvwxyz—9 points

abcdefghijklmnopqrstuvwxyz—10 points

abcdefghijklmnopqrstuvwxyz—12 points

abcdefghijklmnopqrstuvwxyz—14 points

abcdefghijklmnopqrstuvwxyz—18 points

Each type size will call for a larger column width if you follow the advice of the experts.

Easiest Reading Happens at Six Words to a Line

The size type you should use depends on the width of your columns. Some experts have suggested that about six words per line is easiest for the eye to read. This paragraph uses that reasoning. If you stopped to count the words, you would find an average of six per line.

something that is apt to be read, you are more likely to achieve your goal.

Another test of appropriate type size is to look at hyphenation. If the type is too big for the column width, hyphens will abound. Most typesetting professionals advise that 10-point type with 12-point leading is the smallest acceptable type size for larger bodies of text. Try experimenting with column and type size to find a fit that is most comfortable for you and your readers.

Text Alignment

Since the advent of word processors and computers, it has become fashionable to "justify" the text to the margins. This means that the spaces between the letters and words of the line are adjusted so that every line is equal in length. It gives the text a uniform appearance, and thus everything looks tidy.

For years typesetters used full justification, while typists had to leave a ragged right margin. The desktop explosion allowed the average person to copy the style of the professional printer, and everyone did just that. But more recently this has begun to change. Studies now show that most people find it easier to read text when the lines are flush on the left margin and ragged on the right margin. The eye seems to have an easier time picking up words that are predictably spaced. Extra spaces tend to slow down reading. What we have said about the creative use of white space comes into play

here as well. A justified text gives the page a darker look than one that has a ragged right margin. The unevenness tends to leave more white space on the right margin, which gives the page an open look.

There are four basic options for textual alignment. The alignment style you choose will influence the overall look of the page.

Centered Text

Centered text is great for
invitations, announcements, and
short sections of copy that
need to stand out. The page has an
open look because the text
is surrounded by white space. It is
hard to read at any length because
the eyes have to work to find the
next line and guess at the
next word.

Fully Justified Text

Full justification gives a formal look to the text. It is appropriate for work that needs to be kept and filed, like the minutes of meetings and boards. It gives a darker look to the page because it fills the space on the page with type. It can be harder to read because the spaces between words and letters are sometimes adjusted unequally. Many newspapers still use justified text. Full justification allows them to fit more words into a column. More and more newsletter editors are moving away from it today in favor of the open look produced by ragged right alignment.

Justified Left and Ragged Right Aligned Text

This is the most popular style today. Numerous studies reveal that the combination of the open look of the page created by the ragged right edge and the predictability of the justified left margin make this the easiest pattern for the eye to follow. It also uses white space creatively and draws the reader into the article. This alignment style is good for any printed material that aims to sustain the reader's interest for a period of time.

Ragged Left and Justified Right Aligned Text

This option is best reserved for special text. Used for titles, captions, and special effects, it will capture the reader's attention. Used for body copy, it will not be taken seriously.

Paragraph Spacing

Adding a line of space between paragraphs is another way to brighten up the page. It also helps define the individual paragraphs, which encourages the reader to jump in. Look at the two stories on the right.

Notice how much darker the page on the top appears. The justified text, tight spacing between the paragraphs, and lack of white space are very noticeable. The story below is more inviting and easier to read, but notice that less text fits in the box. The same story isn't presented on both pages; less of it appears in the box below. Adding lines of space does make a difference, but you will have to cut the text to fit the available space.

Tabs and Indentation

You may want to indent important points or passages in the text. This technique shapes the text and its message. Many newsletter editors, however, prefer to mark off paragraphs simply by adding a line of space between them. This has the added

The Baptists
by John E. Skoglund

Baptists are Christians who believe in a gathered church that is composed of believers baptized into the name of the Father and the Son and the Holy Spirit.

John Smyth and the Church

In 1602 John Smyth, a brilliant young Cambridge graduate and city preacher at the Anglican Cathedral of Lincoln in England renounced the episcopacy of the established church as being unscriptural from his pulpit. Such preaching brought immediate reaction from the authorities, who had Smyth removed from his lectureship. As a result, he joined a small group of Separatists in Gainsborough, who called him as their pastor. In most respects this group was similar to what has been known more recently as a Congregational church.

When persecution in England became severe, John Smyth's Gainsborough group, along with another Separatist congregation, moved to Holland, and in 1606 his group became the Second English Church at Amsterdam.

John Smyth and the Bible

John Smyth was a purist in almost everything. In 1608 he found himself in the midst of a controversy with the First English Church over the use of translations of the Bible in the worship of God. Such translations, he said, were not the pure word of God, which was to be found only in the untranslated text. Therefore he insisted that all who led in divine worship must be so skillful in Hebrew and Greek as to be able to make their own impromptu translations for the less learned members of their congregations.

Furthermore, he said, no book except the original Scripture should be used in public worship. He held that all psalms sung should be memorized. A psalm book, he declared, stands between man and God. Such rigidness as that of Smyth would indeed be difficult for a congregation.

The Baptists
by John E. Skoglund

Baptists are Christians who believe in a gathered church that is composed of believers baptized into the name of the Father and the Son and the Holy Spirit.

John Smyth and the Church

In 1602 John Smyth, a brilliant young Cambridge graduate and city preacher at the Anglican Cathedral of Lincoln in England renounced the episcopacy of the established church as being unscriptural from his pulpit. Such preaching brought immediate reaction from the authorities, who had Smyth removed from his lectureship. As a result, he joined a small group of Separatists in Gainsborough, who called him as their pastor. In most respects this group was similar to what has been known more recently as a Congregational church.

When persecution in England became severe, John Smyth's Gainsborough group, along with another Separatist congregation, moved to Holland, and in 1606 his group became the Second English Church at Amsterdam.

John Smyth and the Bible

John Smyth was a purist in almost everything. In 1608 he found himself in the midst of a controversy with the First English Church over the use of translations of the Bible in the worship of God. Such translations, he said, were not the pure word of God, which was to be found only in the untranslated text. Therefore he insisted that all who led in divine worship must be so skillful in Hebrew and Greek as to be able to make their own impromptu translations for the less learned members of their congregations.

Notice how the bulleted text below stands out. Not only is each person's name highlighted, but the spacing adds interest to the page. You can also use indentation to highlight items in lists.

benefit, as noted above, of brightening the page.

When you have a long article, tabs and indentation can further open up the story and add white space. Consider the page below. Would it look better if it consisted of a few longer paragraphs? Why or why not?

story and promote a sense of unity and organization on the page.

Look at how the text has been wrapped around the illustration and used to demonstrate a wraparound. Any time you can tie an illustration into your story, it will help the reader visualize what is being said. When it comes to putting a newsletter together, illustrations are not just pretty pictures. They can help you deliver your message. So do not be afraid to incorporate them into the text and get the reader to look at them.

Students Sharing God's Gifts

Many churches hold a student-led service on a regular basis, but it has been many years since we tried to have one here at First Baptist.

We started the new year with Kate Strouse, a freshman at William Smith College in New York, as our guest preacher. She shared with us how God walks with us through the changes in our lives, drawing on her personal experience of going away to school. She pointed to Moses and David and reflected on the fact that God went with them as they faced uncertainty. She then concluded that God will be there for us as well.

Kate's great-grandfather, the Reverend George H. Strouse, would have been pleased to hear her speak.

The other student leaders included:

- Brian Goldin with the children's moment
- Amy Brockway with the pastoral prayer
- Jamie Burgess with a call to worship
- Mikel Brockway with the benediction
- Curt Royce with the responsive reading
- Jeff Brockway, Ben Strouse, and Lauren Royce with the offering

Student Recognition Sunday gave us the chance to tell our young people that we believe in them. It was a great day for everyone. It was a great day and I cannot wait until next time.

Wraparounds

A wraparound is another way to use textual alignment artistically. The text is actually wrapped around photographs and illustrations. This is an excellent way to tie an illustration,

diagram, or chart into an article. It also is an effective way to use space. Wraparounds put the picture into the

Initial Caps

Setting the first letter of the word in display type adds visual appeal and draws the reader into the article. This is known as using an initial cap. There are three basic ways to use an initial cap. It can be raised, dropped, or freestanding. Each style has a different look.

Raised caps extend above the line of text. In this example, the *R* is raised.

Dropped caps cut into the paragraph they introduce, as the *D* illustrates. They can drop as many lines as you wish, not just two, as in this instance.

Freestanding caps are set apart from the text in the left margin to create an interesting visual effect. This paragraph has a freestanding *F*.

Always use letters that are significantly larger than the type of the body text so that you get a real contrast. (Some word-processing programs have a feature that creates dropped caps automatically.) It is the contrast that catches the reader's eye and makes the use of initial caps effective.

Finally, try to set the initial caps as close to the body of text as possible. (Hand kerning may well be necessary here. If you are not entirely sure how to do this, check the manual that came with your word-processing program.) This will look more natural and increase the readability of the text. Page layout programs such as Adobe PageMaker, Quark XPress or Corel Ventura Publisher have features that will automatically insert an initial cap in the appropriate size.

Creating Special Effects with Type

Special effects can add visual interest to your newsletter. Most word processing programs support a variety of special effects and text art.

Stretching and Compressing Type

You can also stretch or expand the type to create headlines and special logos.

Special Effects

Type can be compressed to give an interesting look.

They Are Fun!

Rotating Type

Type can also be rotated to create special effects for nameplates and banners or special announcements.

Textual Land Mines

Manipulating type and molding text can build excitement and add interest to your publication. But there are some land mines to be wary of as you work. They can blow up in your face if you are not careful.

Widows and Orphans

A widow is a partial line of text that stands all alone at the top of a page. It is usually the first line of a new paragraph. An orphan is a partial line of text that stands alone on the bottom of a page.

As we move text around to add white space by inserting lines between paragraphs, we may find ourselves with a host of widows and orphans. They impede reading because the reader has to connect the partial line to the page before or after. Try to keep paragraphs together and avoid leaving orphans and widows.

Rivers of White

Full justification of text may lead to "rivers of white" breaking into the text. Because justification is achieved by manipulating the space between letters and words, some pockets of white space will develop in the text. We noted that the creative use of white space enhances readability. On the other hand, random pockets of white space within the text discourage the reader. If rivers of white develop within the text, go in and manipulate the text

Using the type itself to guide the reader's attention to important paragraphs is an excellent way to make your message jump out at the reader.

•LOOK AT ME!•LOOK AT ME!•

This can be fun for the editor who has some time to experiment and play around. But it can also be helpful in bringing out key messages *if* it is used with discretion.

manually to get rid of them. The judicious use of hyphenation can also relieve exaggerated pockets of white space.

Hyphenation Frenzy

Today many computer programs allow you to hyphenate words automatically. However, do not allow hyphens to break more than three lines in succession. This is distracting to the reader. Be careful and try not to let the automatic hyphenator take over your page. Some consider it poor design to use hyphenation with ragged right text, but some re-writing may be necessary to avoid very short lines within a paragraph.

Come join us!

First Baptist Church is first and foremost affiliated with the American Baptist Churches U.S.A. headquartered at Valley Forge, Pennsylvania.

Over six thousand U.S. Baptist churches and thirty-nine city, state, and regional groups have banded together to carry out a national and international ministry.

We are also a covenanting member of the American Baptist Churches of Connecticut. Out of the Hartford office, 130 churches are united to do mission work in the states and to serve as resources for one another.

Many ministries have evolved over the years, but five specific ministries are very much in the forefront.

Camp Wightman in North Stonington provides conference, camping, and picnic programs that serve over five hundred children, youth, and adults each season as well as numerous other groups and families.

Elderly residents receive excellent care at the Pierce Home, Mills Manor, and the Mystic River Home. Finally, the Noank Baptist Home for Girls offers shelter to teens from distressed families. On the local level, we are also one of twenty-six contributing members of the Stonington Union—New London Association, a gathering of Baptist churches in southeastern Connecticut.

An orphan will confuse the reader here.

Justification can create spaces within a line when word-processing programs won't hyphenate an unknown word.

Rivers of white disrupt the flow of the reader's eye along the lines of copy.

Too many paragraphs of short length can create horizontal bars of white space which disrupt the flow of the story.

Come join us!

First Baptist Church is first and foremost affiliated with the American Baptist Churches U.S.A. headquartered at Valley Forge, Pennsylvania.

Over six thousand U.S. Baptist churches and thirty-nine city, state, and regional groups have banded together to carry out a national and international ministry.

We are also a covenanting member of the American Baptist Churches of Connecticut. Out of the Hartford office, 130 churches are united to do mission work in the states and to serve as resources for one another.

Many ministries have evolved over the years, but five specific ministries are very much in the forefront.

Camp Wightman in North Stonington provides conference, camping, and picnic programs that serve over five hundred children, youth, and adults each season as well as numerous other groups and families.

Elderly residents receive excellent care at the Pierce Home, Mills Manor, and the Mystic River Home. Finally, the Noank Baptist Home for Girls offers shelter to teens from distressed families.

Conclusion

There are some simple techniques that a skillful newsletter editor can employ to make text virtually jump off the page and grab the reader's attention.

When shaping the text for readability, remember the following:

- Column width and type size go hand in hand. Keep them in balance.

- Use the rule of six words per line or an alphabet and a half per column.

- Add a line of space between paragraphs to increase the white space, but remember not to indent the first line if you choose this style.

- Choose a style of line alignment that supports the message you want to send. There are four styles: left, right, center, and full.

- You can use indentation and tabs to shape the text for easier reading.

- You can use wraparounds to integrate text and illustrations, suggesting a visual image of what is being said.

- Initial caps and special effects can attract the reader's interest.

- Watch out for widows and orphans that show up in the text. Be sure to take care of them.

- Be on the lookout for rivers of white and seal them off.

- Beware of hyphen mania.

Using Graphics to Speak for You

What Is a Graphic?

We live in a fast-paced society where people focus on images rather than words. We have been profoundly influenced by television and have embraced the "sound bite"—a single word or image that is used to tell an entire story.

It comes as no surprise that the evening newspaper has given way largely to the evening news broadcast. Around ten years ago, however, *USA Today* challenged the trend away from the print media with a national newspaper.

USA Today uses pictures and images, color and graphics to tell the story of American life. A lot of people scoffed at the newspaper when it first came on the scene, but their laughter has long since died away.

People prefer to look at articles that include graphics. When the mail comes, they look first at the magazines, newspapers, and letters that include pictures and illustrations.

The pictures, cartoons, drawings, and illustrations used in publishing are called graphics. They tell a story without using words. Some can stand alone, while others combine with the text to give the reader a vivid picture of some event or happening.

A graphic can be as simple as a line or a box that helps outline or set off a section of text. A drawing or clip art can serve as a graphic. Anything that is not text but helps tell a story can be used as a graphic.

Using Rules in Desktop Publishing

In the publishing world a rule is not something that you have to follow. A rule is something that sets apart blocks of text. It is the line that separates two competing stories or graphics.

Rules help organize space on a page and help direct the movement of the reader's eye. They bridge the gaps between sections of text.

Notice how the rules are used on this page and the preceding ones. The thick rule at the top of this page separates the chapter title from the body copy below. Look at the parallel horizontal rules on the right. They frame the text of the call out.

Graphic illustrations are key ingredients in putting together newsletters that capture people's attention. Note, however, that overuse of graphics can be distracting. People read text that includes graphics. Use this tool to reach your readers.

59

Why We Need a Crying Room

An Editorial by Dawn Caruso

The property committee has the unique but sometimes difficult charge of adapting our physical environment to our spiritual needs. Most churches desire to have various age-groups represented in their membership. We can learn so much from our older members. We can experience such joy from just one smile from a smaller member. The sign of a healthy church is a mixture of all the age-groups. The sign of a progressive church is the accommodations it makes to help its congregations feel physically comfortable so that they can focus on their spiritual well-being when present.

As we look for ways to make our church grow, the property committee might explore the possibility of integrating a "crying room" in or around our sanctuary. This is a partitioned room where parents can take their young children but still participate in and feel part of the church service.

I recently visited a church whose sanctuary had a two-room annex. The effect was breathtaking. The rooms in the annex served as classrooms, but during the Sunday service they were "crying rooms." They were not soundproof, and they were not elaborate. But parents like them for a variety of reasons.

Many children (take mine for example, please) are simply too young to sit quietly through a service. But I do not feel comfortable having my son talking and chattering during the church service. And Cody is just not comfortable staying with a "stranger" in the nursery.

Another mother mentioned to me that it's such a struggle to rush to dress her children, pack them in the car, and bundle them into the church—just to make it through the first hymn before one of them starts screaming and has to go downstairs. Those in the nursery area cannot hear the service. Even if we were singing at the tops of our voices, the noise could

Look at the newsletter page above. The headline catches our attention, but the graphics draw us in.

Examine the way rules are used in a variety of publications. Newspapers separate columns of text with thin rules. Magazines separate text from advertising with a variety of rules. Books and journals use rules to separate footnotes from text. Most publications use rules.

Before you decide what rule you want to use, look at the other elements on the page. The size of the rule should be consistent with the character of the type and the general page design. Large, bold type needs broad rules to complement it. Smaller, lighter type demands thinner rules.

Generally speaking, a rule should be used to define or punctuate the text

and enhance the other elements on the page. Be careful not to go overboard!

The use of rules is a matter of common sense. If the rule looks good and serves a purpose, then go with it. If all it does is look good, leave it out.

Using Boxes and Borders

Boxes and borders highlight text and draw the reader's attention to it. Whereas rules can guide the reader's attention, boxes scream, "Look at me!"

Use boxes when you want to:

- Emphasize one text over another.
- Break text into shorter paragraphs that are easier to read.
- Create a border around graphics.
- Add interest to a monotonous-looking page.

There are many different types of borders, including simple borders that you can make yourself and fancy borders that come in desktop publishing programs. Plain borders are used to separate. Shadowed borders tend to jump out at the reader. Filled or shaded borders highlight the text. Fancy borders make text very conspicuous. Always take the type and page design into consideration when choosing the box that you want to use.

Boxes and borders are important elements of page design that can help you tell your story. Reserve them for your most important messages. They will be noticed and read.

Plain borders are used
to separate.

Shadowed borders give the
image a raised look.

Background fill highlights
the text.

Using Ornaments or Dingbats

Most type galleries have at least one font that consists of little symbols called dingbats. Zapf dingbats are very well known. They can be used to enhance any newsletter. Look at the following samples.

Zapf Dingbats

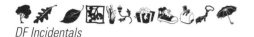

DF Incidentals

Because the dingbats are type, they can be used and manipulated like regular type. They can be enlarged, rotated, tilted, outlined, or shadowed.

Zapf Dingbats Outlined

Always use dingbats with discretion, remembering that their purpose is to help communicate your message. Use the dingbats to punctuate the text or as artwork. Just be careful not to overuse them. Resist the temptation to use everything that is available. Otherwise your readers may lose sight of your message amid the clutter.

Using Artwork

The best way to enhance a story in print is to include a picture with it that graphically portrays what you want to say. An apt graphic illustration speaks volumes and opens the reader's mind. Make sure the illustrations are clearly related to the text so that the reader doesn't have to stop and figure out why they are there.

There are several possible sources of artwork for newsletters.

First, it can be created by an artistic staff member. Drawings can be cut and pasted onto the layout sheet or

scanned onto a disk and imported into the newsletter as it is being created on the computer. If your newsletter does not have an artist in residence, you may be able to hire one.

Most churches cannot afford to hire an illustrator, and many do not have access to an artist. This is where clip art companies have filled a real void. Clip art consists of professionally drawn illustrations that come in collections for use in newsletters, brochures, reports, and pamphlets. These pictures are easy to use and reasonably priced. They can be used to turn an ordinary newsletter into a masterpiece. (Well, almost!)

Clip art can also be combined with other images or it can be cropped or enlarged to create a special effect.

You can combine more than one piece of clip art to create interesting images that build excitement. You stretch it or distort it any way you like. Basically, clip art can be used any way that helps you get your message across.

Some churches hire an artist to work on their newsletter. You may not find this feasible. Clip art publishers have made it possible for everyone to include great graphics in their newsletters. These illustrations are inexpensive and relatively easy to use.

Here is a full picture of a shepherd with some sheep as it was imported onto the page. It can be reduced in size so that it fits into a specific article or cropped to suit special needs.

The Good Shepherd

Charts and graphs can help your reader understand what is happening in the story. They can complement with a visual explanation whatever point you are trying to make.

Some Tips on Purchasing and Using Clip Art

Clip art is available on single sheets, in books, and on computer disks. Decide what format is right for you to use and get started.

- If you buy the sheets or books, it is always a good idea to copy it for use in your publication. Save the originals for future use.

- Clip art images can be scanned onto computer disks, but you should obtain permission from the publisher to do this. Most clip art publishers allow you to make copies for your own personal use.

- Make sure the clip art you purchase on disk is compatible with your computer and your desktop publishing program. Check the information on the outside of the box before you take it to the checkout.

- If you want to edit clip art on disk, you need a paint or drawing program. Most major word processing applications include one. Or the clip art manufacturer can recommend one.

- The images can be cropped, enlarged and rotated. You can manipulate size and shape to make them fit your design.

- There are various styles of clip art. Some resemble line art. Others are more impressionistic. Still others are flashy. Pick the style that best complements your message.

Using Graphs, Charts, and Diagrams

Graphs, charts, and diagrams are informational graphics. They tell a story with information that is incorporated in their design. They are easy to create and can be very impressive.

Graphs and charts show the relationship between two or more variables. Make sure the variables are clearly labeled. Do not assume that a graph will be able to speak for itself. A word of explanation is usually helpful, so include a caption with each chart.

Several types of graphs and charts can be used to help share information. Each one has a slightly different function. A pie chart shows the relationship of all of the parts to the whole. Bar charts make comparisons between variables. Line charts display trends over time.

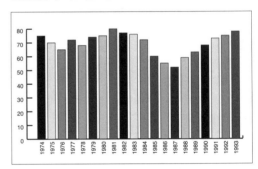

For example, this graph shows average attendance at worship over a period of twenty years.

There are other tools you can use to help the readers sort through complicated information. Diagrams can help the reader understand complex relationships. Flow charts and organizational charts can help the reader understand how key issues are decided.

Time lines can be very helpful in discussions of historical issues. They put things into perspective by linking certain people and events with a time and a place.

Finally, tables can help you explain information in a concise manner. All of the information is gathered and assembled in a way that allows the readers to come to their own conclusions. This is the best way to present data that you want the reader to absorb.

Remember that these are graphics, and the same rules that govern graphic design apply to them. Moderation should be your guiding principle.

Conclusion

Graphics can help send a message to the reader. They add interest and help support what the text is saying. Use them to get your point across.

Be careful not to go wild with graphics. Use them in moderation and only when they help to communicate the written text.

By way of review, the sample on this page includes several elements of graphic design that we touched on in this chapter.

Special Border

Vertical Rule

Clip Art

Boxed Item

Special Thanks to . . .

The Rezendes family for cooking the wonderful breakfast for those who attended the sunrise service this morning. Everyone was delighted with the lovely menu.

Kathy Duntz and the flower committee for their work in organizing the Easter flowers and setting up the beautiful display that is before us. All those taking flowers home should come to the front of the sanctuary following the service this morning.

Adele DiBiagio and the choir for their inspiring music this morning. We have been blessed all year by their faithfulness in God's service.

We also want to thank Amy Brockway and Lori Lord for their instrumental music and Beth Gagnon for sharing her gift of song this morning.

Opportunities to Serve . . .

The fundraising committee has scheduled three future events, and we need willing volunteers to help. Our annual tag sale will be held on June 3,

and we are looking for people to serve on the committee. We are also planning to hold a chicken barbecue on one weekend in July. Finally, we are planning a "pumpkin festival" in early October. There is a sign-up sheet for each activity in the narthex. Thanks in advance for your help!

ABCCONN Annual Meeting

On Saturday, April 29, representatives from 130 American Baptist churches in Connecticut will gather for the annual meeting at First Baptist Church of Meriden. If you would like to go and experience the fellowship and inspiration, speak to the pastor today. We are looking for a few people to represent our church.

Baptist Bowlers

If you are interested in bowling for fun and fellowship on Sunday nights this summer, please sign up in the narthex. We are looking at our fourth season at the Norwich Ten Pin. You can pick your own four-person team or let us fix you up. We bowl from Memorial Day to Labor Day. Talk to Oliver Bray if you want to hear more about it.

Using Photographs

Photography Can Bring Your Newsletter to Life

Any newsletter editor who wants to increase readership should consider adding photographs. Photos are the most effective form of visual communication. A good picture adds immediacy to the story and draws the reader into it. Newsletter articles can help bring people in the congregation together by featuring various members in its pages.

Photographs are effective design elements, since they capture people's attention so well. A well-written article combined with attractive photographs is a real winner.

See how the photo collage on the following page graphically debunks the stereotype that Sunday school is just for kids. The pictures show people of all ages involved in Sunday school activities. You could write a full-page story explaining that your Sunday school is intergenerational, but the pictures prove it.

The effort that you make to bring photographs into your newsletter will reward you with a much more exciting publication.

In this chapter we will discuss the following:

- Finding a photographer
- Finding the right camera and film
- Recognizing photographic opportunities
- Cropping and preparing photos for reproduction
- Organizing photos on the page
- Writing captions

Finding a Photographer

There may be several people in your congregation who enjoy photography as a hobby and would be willing to serve as staff photographers. Or you may find volunteers who simply have a camera and would be glad to take pictures for the newsletter.

Once you have assembled the people who will be taking your photographs, tell them what you are looking for and suggest how they might get results. If money is available, offer to pay for the

Today almost everyone has a camera to take pictures of the family. Recruit some volunteers to share their talent and make the newsletter more appealing.

film and processing. Some volunteers donate these items, but do not assume that they can or they will.

Make your expectations clear to the photographers. Spell out the basics of the story you are working on and explain what kind of illustrations you are looking for. Encourage them to experiment so they can get several photos that might be suitable.

Choosing the Camera and Film

Finding the Right Camera

You do not have to spend a fortune on cameras and special equipment in order to make photography a part of your newsletter production. You can purchase a digital camera and capture your images right on disk, but it is not necessary to go to that expense. If you already have a camera with extra lenses and filters, then you can use that. If

you do not have a fancy camera, then a simple automatic 35 mm camera will suffice. For a modest investment of $99 to $199 you can have a camera that will take excellent pictures.

Important camera features to look for include

- auto-focus lens,
- DX-coding,
- built-in light meter,
- zoom lens.

The auto-focus lens makes getting a clear picture much easier for the novice photographer. The camera does the work of setting up the shot. Make sure that the subject is in the center of the picture to get the best results. Beware of the cheaper imitations of the auto-focus cameras. There are also cameras that are called "focus-free." These cameras are not quite as good because the focus is preset and the range is inflexible.

Who Says Sunday School Is Just for Kids?

The DX coding means that the camera can use all speeds of film, from 50 to 3200. This allows you greater flexibility in choosing film for different occasions. Taking pictures inside with a flash requires higher speed film than shooting outside in bright sunlight. The DX-coded cameras determine the speed necessary and automatically adjust the camera's internal settings.

A built-in light meter lets you know when more light is needed. The flash then works automatically.

The zoom lens helps you focus in on the subject, eliminating unnecessary background objects and getting a nice close-up shot. Close-ups work especially well in newsletters. Try to get a lens that zooms to at least 75 mm (or higher).

If you do decide to purchase a digital camera, make sure that it can handle a resolution of 640 x 480 pixels and hold more than just a few images in its memory. Prices for digital cameras begin at around $200.

Choosing the Right Film

Black-and-white film produces the best photographs for black-and-white newsletters. The only problem you may encounter with black-and-white film is that it is not available everywhere and it can be costly to process. Color film is cheaper and easier to use. If you do decide to use color film because of its convenience, realize that you may lose some quality. You can compensate for this loss by getting excellent shots.

Before you decide what film speed to buy, ask yourself the following questions: What is being photographed? Will the pictures be taken in broad daylight? Will people be photographed in action? Will the photography be done in a large room with poor lighting? A higher film speed is needed as the lighting grows weaker and the action becomes faster. When taking pictures of a sporting event or shooting pictures at night, a higher film speed will

The camera that took the picture of these girls had a built-in zoom lens that allowed the photographer to focus on them.

capture the best shots.

Film with a lower speed will give the sharpest pictures but needs more indirect light for indoor shots. This can be a problem with many automatic cameras. So choose the appropriate film speed for each event. For taking pictures at an outdoor church picnic, choose a 100 speed film. When shooting a baptism or wedding inside, choose a 400 speed film. If the same camera is being used to film both events, then compromise with a 200 speed film.

Shooting the Action

The best pictures for newsletters are ones that show the subjects in action. They tell a story by showing an event in progress. Candid photos show real people doing what the newsletter story describes. Stay away from posed shots and group photos unless there is no alternative.

For example, instead of taking a picture of the pastor sitting behind a desk, shoot one of him or her doing something that shows what ministry is all about. Instead of photographing new members standing in front of the pulpit, get a shot of them being greeted by others. Try getting a picture of what

Second, it will save time later. It is so easy to take a picture and then find out that the background is distracting. The extraneous background must be cropped out, or it can distract the reader's attention from the subject. By focusing in on the subject and filling the whole frame, you can avoid this problem.

Try to get pictures of the subjects looking right at the camera. These photos are great because the subject will appear to be looking right at the reader. Eye contact is established and the reader is drawn to the picture. Eye contact can be as important in print as it is in real life.

Finally, avoid pictures of large groups. These make great mementos but poor newsletter material. People tend to lose their individuality in one large visual image and readers tend to skip the picture.

Cropping the Photos

Cropping photographs refers to cutting out all unessential background by trimming it away. When considering a picture for the newsletter, identify the dominant feature in it. Then decide how to cut out the clutter in the background while keeping the rectangular or square shape.

Cropping the photograph emphasizes the feature that you want to focus on and makes it more useful in illustrating your story. Cropping is important because even the best-planned shots can have unnecessary, distracting objects in the background. Cropping helps put the focus on the main subject of the shot.

Cropping photos molds and shapes them so that they fit into the newsletter article. When designing a certain page, you may want a circular photograph. Another story may need a large square one. Cropping allows you to isolate the dominant feature so that the photo can be enlarged or reduced to fit the parameters of your design needs. A

Special Days   And A Child Shall Lead Them...

Christmas Pageant Featured A "Star" That Involved Us In The Old, Old Story

The play began with Amanda Calkins wishing on a star. In the midst of a busy holiday season, Amanda, Ben Strouse, Amy Brockway and Carolyn Weisbrod encountered *the Star of Bethlehem.* From that point forward the Star explained the real events behind the Christmas celebration.

This year Jessica Hollis and Jonathan Vanase played Mary and Joseph. As the story unfolds they make their way to Bethlehem and encounter three innkeepers before finding one who gives them a place. Then the Star (the voices of April Rezendes and Rebecca Lord) tells of the Angels' visit to the shepherds in a nearby field and their trip to see the child.

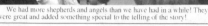

We had more shepherds and angels than we have had in a while! They were great and added something special to the telling of the story!

Allison Walberg greets Santa Claus

135 people came out to enjoy the night which included a Pot-Luck. Our Hall was alive with the sounds of children. Rosie Main calmed them down by reading the story of Saint Nicholas' visit to a home long ago. As the reading ended Santa Claus (C.A.L.) made his entrance bearing gifts for the children. Many of the kids had gifts for Santa to bring to the TVCCA Homeless shelter in return.

Ben Strouse gets a laugh.

Rosie Main continues the tradition of reading to the children that began in 1986 with Len Royce.

Two little angels, Mindy and Kate.

It was a great night and it ended with lots of laughter and joy.

Fellowship Hall was at its capacity for the Party this year.

The photographs in the newsletter above were all taken indoors with a 400 speed film. The 400 speed is faster and needs less light to get a clear shot.

---

happens in Sunday school by photographing the children engaging in a discussion with the teacher or working on a craft. This brings the stories to life and adds interest to the newsletter.

It is also a good idea to get close-ups of the people being photographed. Fill the entire frame with the subject of the picture. Doing this will accomplish two things. First, it helps you capture the personality of the subject and helps the reader identify with him or her. Readers like to know the people they are reading about. If the readers feel a kinship with the subjects, they are more likely to get involved and read the stories.

photograph that has a lot of background material will appear to have even more when it is enlarged and placed on the page. By cropping it before you enlarge it, you will have more of the subject, not more of the background.

The two photos on this page are of the same two girls and take up approximately the same amount of space. The one above has not been cropped, and so the girls are just one part of what we see. There is a lot of background "noise." The picture below has been cropped and enlarged so that the girls fill the whole frame. There is less background, and the focus is on the girls. This is a much better picture for a newsletter.

Reproducing Photos

Poor photo reproduction will result in photos that spoil the appearance of your newsletter rather than enhance it. You have four options available in preparing photos for reproduction.

First, you can have an area print shop convert the photos into halftones. Ask the printer to use a coarse halftone screen, such as one hundred lines per inch. This process turns the photograph into small dots of varying intensity. Halftones are needed to compensate for the inability of most copy machines to distinguish between shades of gray. Pictures that are just copied usually come out dark. Converting a picture into a halftone representation allows the copy machine mechanism to pick up the individual dots and translate them into print. The picture comes out much crisper and with varying degrees of gray.

A second and less costly option is using photo screens. These screens can be purchased from mail-order companies for use in your own office. You lay the screen over a photo and then copy it. The results are not as crisp and clear as halftones, but the quality is nevertheless

The girls make up just one part of the picture above. The reader really has to zoom in to get a good look at them. To the casual observer, they are just two children in front of a door. There is no question as to what the subject is in the second picture. The girls fill the whole frame.

acceptable. These screens have made it possible for most churches to use photographs in newsletters.

A third option is the computer scanner. This device allows you to scan photos into the computer and then import them into your newsletter in a reproducible state. The drawback here is cost, because you need a quality scanner and a laser printer. Dot matrix and ink jet printers with resolutions of

*Using halftones is like
using a shadow to
represent the original. It is
not perfect, but it gives a
pretty good representation
of the original. The
halftone translates the
image into a form that
most copy machines can
reproduce pretty clearly.*

300 dpi (dots per inch) or less will not produce a clear picture even if the scanned image looks great on the computer screen. If your budget allows it, a quality scanner is your best option. Most church newsletters, however, are produced on modest budgets.

A fourth option that is becoming very popular is having the photo shop convert your negatives into digital images and placed on a floppy disk.

Organizing the Photos on the Page

A photograph is the most conspicuous element on a page, and thus it is very important to understand basic principles of design when using photos. Everything we have discussed so far in regard to layout and design applies to photos. But there are some specific points that we need to consider as well.

First, try to position photos so that the subjects' faces are oriented toward the inside of the page, as opposed to looking off the page. Make every effort to arrange the photos so that they help guide the reader's eye over the page.

The smiles on these men's faces give the whole page a friendly feel. Because they are looking to our left, this picture can be used on the right side of the page to direct the reader's attention inward.

men in the photograph in the second column are looking back across the page. This is one way pictures can be organized and used to design the page.

You can also group photos together. Look at the group of photographs on page 66. They are organized to reflect some of the activities that take place in Sunday school. Several related photos can be grouped to make better use of space and create interest. Don't simply pepper pictures across a page.

Size is another element you need to consider. The largest picture is always the most important one, whether it stands alone or in a group. Arrange smaller photos around the dominant one to provide contrast and interest and to support the emphasis of the picture. A row of identically sized pictures is boring to look at. Differing shapes and sizes will add contrast and interest to the page.

Be careful not to overload the page with photographic images. The reader will skim over too many pictures. Employ principles of good page design to make sure the pictures stand out and receive notice.

This photo is a great one to use in a newsletter. It shows the children in action, and their faces show that they are having a good time. Because the children's faces are looking to our right, the picture helps direct the reader's gaze toward the page of text.

Notice how the children in the photograph above are looking in toward the center of the page. The

Writing the Captions

Captions are important and should accompany every picture in the newsletter. They serve to identify the people in the pictures so that the reader can put names with faces. They also explain what the actors are doing and why the picture is important to notice.

People read the captions of the photographs more than any other part of the newsletter except for the major headlines. Pay as much attention to captions as you would a news story. Put the most important facts first. Do not repeat obvious information, but do explain why the image is included. Identify people, places, and the occasion of the photo.

Sometimes a photo and its caption are enough to tell an entire story. In such a case, "a picture is worth a thousand words." You may decide to forgo the article altogether.

Experimenting with Photos

Don't be afraid to experiment with the camera. Try taking pictures from different angles. Try getting close-ups that fill the frame with your subject's face. Try to persuade the subject you are photographing to look right at you. Get a group of people in action. Take a picture of a person in the foreground with something large and symbolic in the background.

As you plan your newsletter, think up ways that pictures can illustrate the stories that are being written. Staged photos can be interesting, but avoid "mug shots." Get a picture of someone doing what is described in the accompanying article.

Most importantly, take a lot of pictures so that you have a selection to choose from. This is the best way to ensure success as you include photos in the newsletter.

Conclusion

Here are tips for good newsletter photographs.

1. Crop out background clutter.
2. Fill the frame with people in action.
3. Capture people looking right at you.
4. Avoid line-up shots. Get people in action.
5. Take pictures of personalities rather than "mug shots."
6. People in the pictures should be looking toward the inside of the page.

Remember:

1. Recruit a staff photographer.
2. Obtain a 35 mm camera and choose appropriate film for picture-taking opportunities.
3. Take pictures of people in action. Fill the frame with a story picture.
4. Crop the photos and cut out the background clutter.
5. Organize the pictures interestingly on the layout sheet.
6. Write exciting and informative captions.

Experiment with your camera. Shoot the picture from different angles. This picture was taken from a vantage point above the workers and gives an interesting look.

Adding Flavor to the News with Interviews

11

Adding Personality to the Newsletter

People like to read stories about people they know. Personal interviews add depth and color to your newsletter and make it seem more personal.

You can use interviews to make your newsletter something readers will look forward to receiving. Interviewing techniques are easy to learn, and the interview itself can be rewarding.

In addition to interviews, profiles or sketches can be used to highlight church members' activities. Profiles and sketches point up important contributions that people have made. They differ from interviews in that the person who is the subject of the profile may or may not be questioned for the article.

Editors who include interviews, profiles, and sketches of special people in their congregations find that the sense of appreciation and recognition expressed in these paragraphs often rubs off on countless others. These profiles say that the church recognizes and appreciates the contributions of its members.

Choosing the Person to Be Interviewed

The list of candidates for interviews is almost endless. An interview is a great way to introduce new members to the church family. An interview with a new pastor or staff member can allow that person to talk about expectations and hopes for the ministry. An interview or a profile of someone who has served in one church position for many years is a nice way to recognize that service. Long-time members of the congregation can describe church life "way back when." Interviews can be employed to highlight and celebrate the many activities and ministries of the church.

Finding an Interviewer

Mike Wallace of the television broadcast *Sixty Minutes* is not the only one who can do an interview. Anyone who likes people and has the time and enthusiasm to visit can do the job. It is a great opportunity for outgoing members looking for opportunities to share their gifts. An interviewer also

Adding interviews to the newsletter will make it feel more personal. Your readers will soon look forward to articles about their friends and neighbors.

creates another member-to-member connection within the congregation. The only skills needed are openness to the interviewee and the ability to listen and take notes. Everything else can be learned very easily.

Planning for the Meeting

Planning and preparation are the key elements in successful interviews. The process begins with a phone call to the subject of the interview to set up a time for the appointment. Specify how long the interview will last and ask the person to think about the aspect of ministry that will be the focus of the interview. This will allow her or him to prepare for the interview. If you plan to have a photograph accompany the interview, ask the person to provide one or get permission to take a picture during the interview.

When deciding what questions to ask, think about the people who will read this interview. What will they find interesting about this person? What do the people in the parish want to know? What would inspire or excite them when they read this article?

The two variables of the interviewee's experience and the reader's interest go hand in hand when conducting and writing an interview for the newsletter. It goes right back to the purpose of the church newsletter. Why are interviews included? The answer should be to further the goals and purpose of the newsletter mission.

What You Need for the Appointment

Before setting off for the interview, gather the necessary tools for the job: pencils, notepad, cassette recorder and batteries, camera and film, and a list of questions.

Using a cassette recorder to tape the interview is a good idea. Always ask the person's permission before taping. The tape recorder allows the interviewer

Planning and preparing for the interview is important. Do your homework before you meet the person for the interview. It is always a good idea to get permission before writing anything personal.

the freedom to take fewer notes and to concentrate more intently on listening to the person. It is difficult to listen to a person when taking notes. It is distracting to the interviewee as well because it interrupts eye contact and rapport. The cassette recorder allows the interviewer to listen and take brief notes on the highlights of the interview. You can draw direct quotes from the tape as you write the article.

Coming prepared demonstrates respect and tells the person that you value the opportunity to interview him or her.

Holding the Interview

Arrive on time and begin the interview by setting the person at ease. Try to establish rapport by finding some common ground. Then thank the person for agreeing to be interviewed and begin with the questions.

To establish a foundation for the later questions, begin with the straightforward factual questions. Then shift to the focus of the interview and move on from there.

Here are some interviewing tips:

- **Keep questions brief and ask them one at a time.**
  Try not to combine a series of questions that call for several answers all in one. Ask short questions that get to the point. It may be tempting to ask several questions in a row, especially if the person does not answer right away. Allow the person plenty of time to think of an answer before you pop the next question.

- **Ask open-ended questions.**
  Stay away from questions that allow for simple yes or no answers. Such replies do not tell what a person thinks or feels and do not contribute to an interesting interview. Ask questions that allow the person to share personal thoughts and feelings. Don't ask questions that have an answer built into them. Sometimes

people will tell you what they think you want to hear. Open-ended questions do not offer the interviewer's thoughts on the subject.

- **Do not interrupt as the person is answering your question.**
Let the person being interviewed do most of the talking. It is easy to take over and begin answering your own questions. Keep your thoughts to yourself. You are the interviewer, not the interviewee.

- **Watch for nonverbal communication.**
People often express themselves through body posture and movements. Look for clues like lip biting or shifting in the seat that may express something that is not being said. Try to persuade the person to verbalize what he or she is feeling or thinking.

- **Do not assume anything. Ask questions that clarify what is said or is not said.**
Do not play mind reader and guess what the person is thinking or means by a comment. If you are not sure you got it right, ask for clarification.

- **Watch the clock and end on time.**
Be faithful to the time commitment you made when you set up the interview. Express your gratitude for the interviewee's cooperation.

Writing Up the Interview

It is important to write up the interview while everything is still fresh in your mind. Begin by identifying an organizing principle around which you can construct the story. The interview does not have to be a chronological record of questions and answers. It can begin with a statement about the person and then move into the focus of the interview. Quotes and notes from the interview can be filtered appropriately into the story to back up and reinforce statements that are made.

As in other articles, the first sentence is the most important one. It will either draw your readers into the story or help them decide to skip over it. The lead sentence in an interview or a profile needs to come from the heart of the story for feeling. It can be a statement about why the person is being featured. It can be a moving quote by the person. It can relate an interesting moment in the person's life. It is important to give plenty of thought to the lead, since it sets the tone for the entire article.

A word of warning: As you are writing the story, try to keep your opinion out of it. It is always tempting to tell the readers what we think or how we feel about the interviewee; however, readers want to know about the person in the profile, not the one who wrote it.

Finally, end the story on a positive note. Either sum up the interview with a few words or lift up an inspiring quote that tells the reader something good about the person. Let the conclusion be a benediction.

Write up the interview while it is still fresh in your mind. Consult with the editor to make sure you don't say anything that could be embarrasing to the interviewee. If you wait until the deadline approaches, you will lose some of your original enthusiasm.

No Mug Shots Please

If you plan to have a photo accompany the article, avoid "mug shots." Try to get a picture in pleasant, natural settings. Smiling, happy faces make readers more receptive to the article.

This photograph shows mother and daughter and gives you a clue about what is important to them. They are both smiling and looking right at the camera.

Conclusion

Adding interviews to the newsletter can be fun and satisfying. Keep the following tips in mind for the best results:

- Use the interviews to recognize outstanding contributions or to introduce members of the congregation.

- Do your homework before the interview. Compile a list of open-ended questions and identify a focus for the interview.

- Gather the tools you need and arrive for the interview on time.

- Ask questions and then listen to the answers. Ask permission to tape the interview so that you can pay full attention to the interviewee.

- Find a key statement or event around which to build the story. Use a mix of facts and quotes to make the story interesting.

- Write up the interview while it is still fresh in your mind. Use the tape recording to fill in gaps and to reproduce quotes accurately.

- Include a photograph showing the person in a natural setting.

Editing, Proofing, and Preparing Final Copy

12

Editing the News

All of the writing, rewriting, and paste-up is done. The newsletter is nearing completion, but one more step remains before the newsletter is actually ready for duplication and distribution.

The newsletter needs to be edited, proofread, and corrected. In many churches one person is responsible for all of these tasks. If the same person also wrote the articles, it may be difficult for him or her to keep an objective perspective throughout the editorial process.

Try to find volunteers to help with copyediting and proofreading. Objective opinions at this stage of the process work to enhance the whole effort by picking up inadvertent errors and omissions. Otherwise your readers will discover them.

There are three parts to the process: editing for content, copyediting for the mechanics of language (grammar, punctuation, capitalization, etc.), and proofreading for errors.

The Content Editor

The content editor will be working on the newsletter from start to finish. The job begins with planning and choosing articles for the current edition. In assigning articles and working on a preliminary layout, the content editor will decide what goes where, how long each article will be, and whether permission is needed for any material.

The hardest part of the job is making decisions on the stories submitted by the various reporters, boards, and committees. The writers may tell you how good their reports are or stress the importance of their news. Make sure writers know that all articles will be edited for style and content so that everyone knows it is nothing personal. Then talk with each of the writers when planning the stories and make sure that they understand the focus of their articles.

Editing is always easier if you can prevent problems before they occur. As the editor, you have to decide if the submission meets your goal and helps serve the people you are writing for. You have the responsibility for judging

Computers have made the process of editing and proofreading much easier, but they have not eliminated the need to do the work. As much as we may love our computers, they cannot make all of the corrections. An editor and a proofreader are still essential volunteers needed in the publication of written material.

the appropriateness of the content of each article.

It is important to be diplomatic in the process but to stand firm in making editorial decisions. If the decisions are made based on timeliness, available space, and the appropriate nature of the stories, the best interests of the church and the readers will be served. It is important to make this clear right at the beginning. Then everyone will have an understanding of the goals and what is wanted and expected.

There is no hard-and-fast rule that says a newsletter must have a certain number of pages. That is the decision of each editor. The number of pages will be determined by the amount of news and the types of stories that will be included. Chapter 3 provides a discussion of the planning process and offers a number of suggestions for content.

The key issue for the editor is space versus content. He or she needs to be aware of the fact that there is only so much space available. Including more material will mean adding more pages and increasing the cost and time necessary to prepare the newsletter. This has to be factored into the decision-making process. Finding the right balance is as essential here as it is in every other aspect of creating a readable newsletter.

Copyright Laws and Seeking Permission

As you prepare your church newsletter, you will probably find articles, illustrations, cartoons, and so forth that may be perfect for your church audience and that you would like to reprint. Knowing copyright basics and following the guidelines are critical when you wish to reprint any material.

According to the U.S. Copyright Office, Library of Congress, in Circular 1, "Copyright Basics" (June 1995), copyright is a statement of governmental protection to the authors of original literary, dramatic, musical, artistic, and certain other intellectual works. This protection is available to both published and unpublished works. Copyrightable works include the following categories: literary works (including computer programs and most "compilations"); musical works, including any accompanying music; pantomimes and choreographic works; and pictorial, graphic, and sculptural works (including maps and architectural works). Copyright laws protect authors of original material from the use of their material without permission. These laws allow the writer, artist, and musician to benefit from their efforts and protect their right to make a profit from their work.

Also according to the Copyright Office, the following are generally not protected by copyright: titles, names, short phrases and slogans; familiar symbols or designs; mere variations to typographic ornamentation, lettering, or coloring; mere listings of ingredients or contents; ideas, procedures, methods, systems, processes, concepts, principles, discoveries, or devices, as distinguished from a description, explanation, or illustration; and works consisting entirely of information that is common property and containing no original authorship (for example: standard calendars, height and weight charts, tape measures and rulers, and lists of tables taken from public documents or common sources).

Questions regarding copyright laws can be directed to the Copyright Office, Library of Congress, Washington, D.C. 20559-6000; 202-707-3000. You can also request Circular 1, "Copyright Basics," and Circular 2, "Publications on Copyright," which provide additional detailed information on current copyright law.

It is important to know when to request permission to reprint any material. There are times when you are not required to request permission to use another's material, but you are

---

The decision of what goes into the newsletter should be based on the timeliness of the article, the availability of space, and the appropriateness of the story. Make this clear right at the outset and it will minimize your worries.

always required to cite the ownership and source of the material.

One example of when you do not have to request permission is when the material is in "public domain." Material becomes part of public domain when the claim of copyright ownership on it has expired. The material can then be used without permission. It is important, though, to continue to cite the material so that others will know your source.

Check your source for guidance on whether the material is in public domain. The copyright page gives the original date of publication and information on later editions or printings. A hymnbook will give a credit line for music that the publisher had to get permission for. If permission was needed to put it in the hymnbook, then you also need to get permission from the credited source. Likewise, if a book's footnote or endnote or copyright page states "used by permission," then you will also need to get permission from the original source.

The Copyright Act of 1976 (effective Jan. 1, 1978) is the current foundation of copyright law. Earlier law allowed a work to be copyrighted for a total of fifty-six years (including renewal) from the date of publication; then it went into public domain. In 1962, works in the second term of renewal had their copyright extended until 1/1/78. Most works published in the United States more than seventy-five years ago can be assumed to be in public domain. Anything published after 1978 is under copyright for "life of the author plus fifty years." For exceptions to this general rule, see *The Chicago Manual of Style, 14th Edition*, which is available at most libraries.

Another exception to having to request permission to use material is the "Fair Use" qualification. Fair use covers the use of much of quoted nonfiction and is the determining factor in seeking permission. No permission is needed for something deemed to be fair use. Generally, use of copyrighted materials for "criticism, comment, news reporting, teaching, scholarship, or research" is considered to be fair use. This definition, however, serves only as a guide; exceptions exist. The following must be considered in determining fair use:

1. Is the work to be used for commercial (is not fair use, permission is necessary, often a fee is required) or nonprofit educational (generally, but not always fair use) purpose?
2. The nature of the copyrighted work (poetry, prose, fiction, nonfiction, etc.).
3. Proportionality: what is the proportion of the quoted material in relation to the whole copyrighted work? (One verse of a 4-verse poem is 25 percent of the whole work; 500 words from a 50,000-word book is merely 1 percent.)
4. The effect of your use of the work upon the potential market for, or value of, the copyrighted work. (In other words, will your use of the work decrease the value of the original?)

In your newsletter, you might find yourself critiquing or reviewing a book, and you might want to reprint a few lines to go with your review. In this case, your quotation could be considered to be fair use. Make sure to transcribe the material accurately (word-for-word, letter-for-letter, comma-for-comma). Do not take the material out of context, and always give credit to the source by using a footnote or endnote.

If you ever doubt whether or not the material you wish to reprint is in public domain or is fair use, you must ask. Contact the original author, artist, publisher, etc., and let them determine if the material can be reprinted.

Jesus built his ministry around the idea that we should love and respect our neighbors. Copyright laws recognize our neighbor's gifts and talents and force us to give them the credit. Churches should be at the forefront of the movement to respect and honor others' rights.

Copyright violation is a serious offense and judges will not accept the excuse that there was not time to get permission. If you want to use copyrighted material, plan ahead and get permission.

When you do need to ask for permission, you should contact the owner of the copyright and detail the exact material you would like to reprint, the publication you would like to reprint it in, the cost of your publication (or no cost), the distribution size of your publication, and why you want to reprint the material (how it enhances the publication). Generally, permission is granted from the copyright owner(s) or publisher without a fee for not-for-profit organizations and publications. Regardless of whether you pay a fee or not, you must always include a credit line to cite the original author of the material, the title of the work from which the material came, the copyright owner (either the publisher or the author), the copyright date, location of publication, and "used by permission."

The U.S. government does not view copyright violation as a frivolous matter. The right to create and own personal property is a part of the American way of life. The penalties for copyright violation are very severe. The law says that damages for infringing upon another's rights will cost a minimum of $250 to a maximum of $50,000 per copy. Add lawyer's fees to this and you are not talking about small change. If the moral convictions will not dissuade you from infringing upon another's copyright, then maybe the financial consequences will. Use other people's materials with their permission, and give them the glory and the credit they deserve.

Copyediting and Proofreading

Copyediting is a useful step to include in your publication process. Perhaps your church is fortunate enough to have a person with copyediting experience who is willing to copyedit the newsletter before each issue is finished. (An experienced English teacher might also be willing and able

to fulfill this responsibility.)

A copyeditor reads for correct grammar and consistency of style—the mechanics of the language. This includes spelling, capitalization, punctuation, use of italics, and so forth. (Make sure the spell checker has been run if you are using a computer.) Of course, if a sentence is unclear or if there are major organizational problems in a piece, the copyeditor can also either point out these problems to the editor or be given the responsibility for correcting them. The copyediting step will reduce the length of time needed for straight proofreading. Generally, the copyeditor assumes that information in articles is accurate. The final responsibility for accuracy rests with the editor, so steps should be taken throughout the process to verify names, dates, times, and other details.

A copyeditor should keep in mind that this is not the time to rewrite a whole piece (unless it is absolutely necessary). A writer's style can usually be preserved while necessary corrections are made. It is helpful to keep in mind the distinction between changing something as a matter of personal preference (word choice, for example) and correcting outright errors. The latter should be the focus of the copyeditor's work. Of course, by using the best writers available for major articles and interviews, an editor can make this step and the overall job of editing go more smoothly.

If there is no one available to do the copyediting, the editor will have the primary responsibility for correctness and should share that responsibility with a proofreader. A proofreading step is absolutely essential (whether the text has been copyedited or not), with the proofreading being done preferably by someone other than the editor or the copyeditor. It's very easy to miss obvious mechanical errors if you've read the material several times for content.

Try to use a proofreader who has had some experience. A proofreader should read word by word, line by line, all of the text in the newsletter. Other important details for the proofreader to check are: headlines, subheads, and captions; spelling of names (correct spelling of names should be stressed from the beginning stage of writing); and numbers and dates. A dictionary is a helpful tool to keep handy. There is some overlap between the work of the copyeditor and proofreader. If the material has been copyedited, there should be far fewer errors for the proofreader to find, but the proofreading step is still essential.

Conclusion

The final step should be to check to see that the proofreader's corrections have been made properly and that no new errors have been introduced. This step should also include checking the placement of graphics and overall design. If you come across errors and omissions after the newsletter has been published, make a note of them and keep an eye out for the same types of mistakes when proofing the next issue. Chances are that the most common mistakes (such as spacing, italicizing, misspelling of names, and so on) will keep coming up.

It's important not to let proofreading become an obsession! Everyone involved in this part of the publication process should realize that perfection is not the goal and that occasional errors are a fact of life for any publication. Once the job has been done to the best of everyone's ability, celebrate the accomplishment of once again sharing a vital message as part of the church family's ministry.

The relationship between the editor and the writer should not be antagonistic. A good editor will raise questions that will help writers get their message across to the reader. The proofreader brings a fresh set of eyes to the page and can help by picking up mistakes and omissions.

Printing and Duplicating the Newsletter

13

Printing the Newsletter

The first step in duplicating the newsletter is getting a print of the final copy. If you used a typewriter to produce the newsletter, that print will come fresh off the roller. Clip art and any other graphics are then added by hand. A final copy is ready when everything is pasted in place.

When you work on a typewriter, you see the final copy as it is being typed. This is truly a "what you see is what you get" production. If you produce your newsletter on a computer, the print comes out of the printer. The quality of the print depends entirely on the kind of printer you use.

Printer Language

Computer printers work by combining hundreds of tiny dots to form images. To evaluate a printer, find out how many dots per inch (dpi) it produces. The more dots per square inch a printer can produce, the more crisp and clear the images will be.

There are three basic types of printers available today.

Dot Matrix Printers

Dot matrix printers were among the first to be made available to the public at a reasonable cost. The use of "dot technology" allowed the user to create and utilize graphics as well as type. These printers are not widely available today. Advances in technology produced better printers even as prices fell, squeezing the inferior dot matrix printers out of the market.

Most dot matrix printers can print at only 72 dpi, and the type comes out looking rough around the edges. If you are still using one of these printers, it will do just fine. There are some software programs that will enhance the quality of the printing. Adobe Type Manager and Bitstream Facelift are very good and not too expensive. On the other hand, now may be the time to consider upgrading your printer. A new printer with a higher print resolution of, say, 600 dpi will enhance the appearance of your newsletter and justify the time and effort you put into producing it.

When they were first introduced, dot matrix printers made a splash by allowing computer users to integrate graphics into their presentations. Today, at an average of 72 dpi, the resolution offered by most dot matrix printers is not really adequate for most printing needs.

Ink Jet Printers

Ink jet printers are a remarkable improvement over the old dot matrix printers. Some of them produce prints that are nearly as good as the ones made by the more expensive laser printer. Most of them produce a print resolution of 600 dpi or higher. Ink jet printers do a very good job with standard type and most graphics. Scanned photographs may not come out as well because the print resolution is not high enough to pick up the differences in shading.

You can produce a high-quality newsletter using an ink jet printer. On the other hand, if you wait a little bit longer, you may be able to afford to upgrade to a laser printer.

Laser Printers

Laser printers produce clear, crisp copies. Photo images, graphics, and type come out bright and clean. Low-end laser printers produce a print resolution of 300 dpi. The price of a laser printer goes up with the print resolution of the output.

The laser printer works by translating data that is transmitted to it by the computer into its own special language. Then it fires a beam of magnetically charged ions onto the page in the form of the text or images. It then releases oppositely charged toner particles onto the paper, which stick to the charged areas. There are two basic types of laser printers. The bitmap laser printer gives a print quality that is far better than the ink jet printer. The postscript laser printer is the best of them all. Cost is usually the factor that determines which printer the church acquires for its office.

Laser printers are much more expensive than dot matrix or ink jet printers. But the difference in quality is readily apparent. If you can buy a good laser printer, it will truly make a difference in the appearance of your newsletter.

Duplicating the Newsletter

You have five options for duplicating your newsletter. Each option has its advantages and disadvantages. Choose the one that best suits your needs and circumstances.

The Computer Printer

The easiest method of duplicating your newsletters is to simply run the number of copies you need off your printer. If you are going to print one copy, you can easily print fifty or a hundred. There are a few things to consider before choosing the computer printer to do all the duplicating work. The cost, wear and tear on the printer, and time needed to produce each issue will be significant. If you need to make up to fifty copies of a one-page newsletter, this method may be the best choice for you. If you need to produce more than fifty copies, you will want to consider a different printing method. Less expensive printers are not built to handle massive volumes and can break down when pushed. The consumable materials may not seem very expensive initially, but costs add up quickly.

Some computers will not let you work on anything else while the printer is active. This could produce some "dead" time in the office as you wait for the computer to be free.

The Mimeograph Machine

I hesitate to even mention this option since most churches have gotten rid of their "old standby" and found another way to print their material. For years the mimeo machine was used to produce bulletins and newsletters in most churches.

In the past, a stencil was "cut" on the typewriter and then placed on the mimeo machine. As the drum turned around, ink was squeezed through the holes that the typewriter keys cut in the stencil, and the image was printed onto the paper. You could produce fifty or a thousand copies at roughly the same cost. Mimeos were popular because they were inexpensive and easy to set up and operate.

You can still obtain the old mimeograph machine. It works well for very large runs. The cost is minimal, and it is a do-it-yourself operation from production to clean-up and maintenance.

There are a few things to consider before deciding to use this option. Parts and service are becoming hard to find as time goes on. The mimeograph is becoming something of a technological orphan. If you need help servicing your mimeo, you may run into trouble in the future. Another consideration is that the stencils can be messy. Ink is likely to get on the operator as well as the paper. Nevertheless, this is the least expensive method of producing large numbers of copies, and start-up costs and supplies are very inexpensive. Clean-up can be performed by the staff.

Digital Duplicators

Digital duplicators combine an electronic scanner and a mimeograph machine under the control of a computer. You insert the page you want to copy into the machine, and it makes a stencil. Copies are then produced from the stencil. The more copies you make, the more cost effective the whole process becomes. Digital duplicators run at very high speeds and have eliminated the mess associated with mimeograph machines.

If you have thoughts of acquiring a digital duplicator, you may want to consider the following:

1. The digital duplicator costs more than most office copiers, although it is much less expensive to run and maintain over the years.

2. It reproduces copies very quickly. A thousand copies can be made in a relatively short time.

3. The cost per copy is very low and decreases with the number of copies made. For churches that regularly produce several hundred copies of the newsletter, the savings really add up.

4. The duplicators have low maintenance costs. They are very durable and have a life expectancy of more than ten years.

5. Working with ink can still be messy. There can be blotting problems and an occasional inking problem.

Office Copy Machines

Nothing beats an office copy machine for ease and access. Office copiers are clean and produce great-looking copies when they are taken care of. If you need one copy or even a few dozen, producing them on the copy machine can be the most cost-effective method. If you are thinking about acquiring a copy machine for your church, you will want to consider the following factors:

1. A good copy machine can be expensive to purchase and will last only three to five years on average. This life may be extended if the machine is not overused.

2. The cost per copy can be about twice that of the mimeograph or digital duplicator. If the copy machine would be used for other purposes as well, however, it might be worth the investment.

3. The copy machine makes up to fifty copies as cost effectively as any other method. How many copies are you going to be making at one time? If more, you may want to consider a different method.

4. The copy machine produces clean, crisp copies whenever they are needed. It allows you to control the timing and delivery of the finished product. This factor is the one that often outweighs all others for those who choose to use the copy machine.

You can produce the newsletter on your printer, but it is not recommended. The wear and tear would shorten the life of the printer considerably. There are better alternatives.

Digital duplicators combine the ease of an office copy machine with the cost effectiveness of a mimeograph machine. They are terrific if you produce a large volume of copies and can afford the original purchase price.

5. Regular maintenance is essential for clean copies. With each copy that is made, the quality goes down ever so slightly. Regular cleanings and tune-ups are necessary to assure quality. Maintenance is not cheap.

Going to the Printer

Offset printing is the fifth option. It involves making a copy of the page on a plate that is used to produce the copies. Offset printing gives a professional look to the page and allows the best use of photography and clean graphics. It also leaves the task of reproducing the newsletter to outside staff and frees up the church office.

Is this option for you? There are a few things to consider:

1. There are no start-up costs. The per-copy expense is slightly higher, but when the price of equipment is factored in, this disappears rather quickly.

2. The printer does the work. All those last-minute problems are taken off your hands. Once you deliver the camera-ready copy, the job is in the printer's hands. You only need to pick up the finished product.

3. Strict adherence to deadlines is a must. In order to keep things rolling along on time, you and the staff need to set deadlines and stick to them. Any delay will cause the whole process to break down.

4. Planning is essential. Everything must be detailed and set up in advance for the printer. Once a copy is shipped, it is in its final form. No last-minute changes!

5. The printer has the tools and technology to get the job done right. You will enjoy a professional-quality product.

Conclusion

There are several factors to consider when choosing among printing and duplicating options.

1. Price: How much can you afford to spend?

2. Ease and convenience: How much time and energy can you spare?

3. Personal preference: Do you like one option over another?

4. What you already have: Does it work? Then keep using it!

Distribution: Sharing the Good News

Reaching the Goal

The most important aspect of newsletter production comes at the very end of the process. Remember that the overarching goal of the newsletter is to share the good news of what is happening in your church. All the work of writing, editing, and printing the newsletter comes to nought if the paper never reaches the audience it was written for.

The same diligence required to pull the newsletter together needs to go into distribution. You have several options to choose from for distribution of your newsletter. The choice each editor makes depends on the goals that were set at the beginning of the process. Who are your readers? What do they need to know and when do they need to know it? How often will you publish your newsletter? What kind of budget do you have?

As you answer these questions, the best method to distribute your newsletter will become clear to you.

Hand Delivery and Community Drop-offs

If the newsletter is intended to promote a greater awareness of the church and its various ministries, it can be distributed like a leaflet or a flyer. It can be left at drop-off sites in the neighborhood or the wider community. Volunteers can also pass the newsletters out door to door while they are canvassing the neighborhood.

Plan to visit areas where there is a heavy concentration of people and find convenient spots to leave or distribute the newsletters. Do not just leave the newsletters at any drop-off site, such as a supermarket lobby, without asking permission of the store owner or manager. This personal contact will help insure that the newsletters are not simply put aside, scattered, or, worse, thrown out. Come back after a few days and see if people are picking them up.

If the newsletters are distributed door to door, do not put them in people's mailboxes. This is illegal. Instead, leave them on the doorstep or in another conspicuous place.

Choosing the best way to get the newsletters to your readership can seem very confusing. There are so many options. You need to begin by reviewing your purpose in producing the newsletter and match it to the option that distributes it most efficiently.

Distribution at Church

If the goal of the newsletter is to inform the active church membership of upcoming activities, it can be passed out at church on Sunday mornings. The papers can be left on a table in a central location, distributed before the service with the worship bulletins, or handed out as people leave the church.

Passing out the newsletters this way will save on postage. The newsletters will also reach the intended readers at a highly receptive moment.

The problem associated with this method of getting the news out is obvious. There will always be some people missing from church on any particular Sunday, and they will also miss the newsletter. Some churches solve this problem by addressing every newsletter and mailing only the ones that are not picked up.

A second problem arises when people forgetfully leave the newsletter behind in the pew after church.

Postal Service

The best way to insure that a newsletter gets to your readership is to mail it. It is also the most expensive way. Postage rates have continued to climb over the years, and there is no end in sight. Still, the price seems like a bargain when compared to the work that would be required to hand deliver each newsletter (if that were even possible).

First-Class Delivery

Mailing the newsletter first class is the most expensive way to send it, but it is also the fastest. This is the best method of distribution for smaller congregations and larger churches that need to inform active church members about news that pertains to the immediate future. First-class mail service will ensure a midweek delivery to everyone on the list, even those living out of town. Everyone is sure to receive advance notice of news and events.

Do not just leave the newsletters at any drop-off site, such as a supermarket lobby, without asking permission.... Personal contact will help insure that the newsletters are not simply put aside, scattered, or, worse, thrown out.

First class is the only postal delivery option for groups that do mailings of fewer than two hundred pieces. If you do mailings of over two hundred pieces, you may want to look into second- or third-class rates.

There is a downside to mailing first class. The cost per piece is based on the weight of each piece. If the newsletter is several pages long and weighs more than one ounce, the cost of mailing it rises dramatically. It might benefit you to increase the size of the mailing and send it second or third class.

Third-Class or Bulk-Rate Delivery

Many churches use the newsletter as a church ambassador and send copies to a long list of people, including active members, former members, newcomers, and prospective members. Since the list is long and the reasons for sending the newsletter are varied, many churches look for a discount rate. The most popular discount rate is third class. It has the fewest restrictions, and the postal service tries to achieve rapid local delivery for nonprofit organizations.

The following qualifications must be met in order to mail the newsletters third class:

- There must be at least two hundred identical pieces per mailing.
- You must obtain a permit, and you must bring the mailing to the same post office each time.
- The newsletters have to be presorted by ZIP code and bundled before they arrive at the post office.
- Other organizations or businesses cannot include advertising inserts in the mailing.

You can save more money if you meet a few additional conditions. For example, adding the ZIP + 4 codes earns an additional price break. If you sort the mail by carrier route or by the three- or five- digit ZIP codes, the rates are even a little cheaper. It is also possible to save money by adding bar codes to the mailing labels.

Generally, the more work you do, the lower your mailing rate. Seminars that teach groups how to take advantage of these savings are offered in every community. Check with the local post office to see when the next class will be held in your area.

The only drawback with third-class mailing is the potential for slow and belated delivery. Even though the postal service tries to deliver mail quickly, third-class mail is always handled after first-class mail. During the busy times of the year, the newsletters may sit for a day or two before getting delivered.

Second-Class Delivery

Larger churches may want to consider using the second-class delivery system to mail their newsletters. The postage rates are reduced, but the qualifications for mailing are stricter. Second-class mailing is generally reserved for trade and business publications that people subscribe to. Churches can take advantage of this option because the newsletters are sent to active members who are supporters, and therefore subscribers, of the news. In order to send the newsletter second class, you must meet the following criteria:

- You must mail the newsletter at least four times a year on a strict schedule.

- You can add special editions, but you must notify the postal service in advance in writing.

- The newsletter must be printed on an offset press or a letterpress.

- Papers printed on a mimeograph machine or an office copier will not be accepted.

- The recipients must request or pay for the subscription. If the newsletter is supported by members' offerings or dues, it can qualify.

- There is no minimum number of copies, but only 10 percent of the total subscription can go to nonpaying members.

- All advertising must be an integral part of the mailing. No inserts or circulars can be included.

- The newsletters must be presorted by ZIP code.

These rules may be too much for the average congregation. Each church needs to determine if the savings are worth the extra time and effort that it takes to get the mailing ready for distribution. When the budget is tight and volunteer energy is high, it may be well worth the effort to apply for the discount rates.

Conclusion

The ultimate goal of every newsletter editor is to get the news to the readers. There are several ways to do that. Choose the method that helps you achieve the result you want!

Think of your readership and then identify the best means of getting the newsletter into their hands. If you need the complete postal instructions and regulations to make a decision, they are available at no cost from your local post office.

Handing out the newsletter at church may be the most efficient means of getting news to active members, but some editors like to send it through the mail just to establish a midweek connection to the church. Mailing the newsletters puts the responsibility for delivery on the shoulders of the postal service. You can save money by doing some preparation, but the letter carriers will do all of the legwork.

Conclusion

A church newsletter can take the good news of your ministry activities to the people in God's churches. Your church newsletter can be an asset that will build up your ministry.

The advent of the personal computer and desktop publishing software has added vigor and excitement to the production of all church publications. Graphics, illustrations, and photographs make the newsletter pages interesting to look at and easier to read.

Anyone can produce well-designed publications that will enhance your church's ministry. Nearly every desktop publishing package includes templates that offer the user a choice of ready-to-use newsletter designs. Those who want to design and lay out their newsletter from scratch will find help in the principles discussed in chapters 4, 5, and 8.

Clip art, computer graphics, and image scanners make it simple to integrate photographs and artwork into a publication. The prices of hardware and software have fallen, making it possible for nearly every church to purchase or lease the equipment needed to put out a professional-looking newsletter.

The church newsletter will be whatever you decide to make it, as you describe your ministry, share news and notes, and tell about the events that make up your life together as a community.

Annotated Bibliography

Ames, Steven E. *Elements of Newspaper Design*. New York: Praeger Publishers, 1989.

This book covers every aspect of newspaper design from the basics to the finishing touches. It is a valuable resource for newsletter editors because it shows how the "professionals" do it. Several examples of newspapers are included.

Brigham, Nancy, Maria Catalfio and Dick Cluster. *How to Do Leaflets, Newsletters & Newspapers*. Detroit, Mich: PEP Publishers, 1991.

This booklet is a general handbook on how to produce all kinds of publications. It is not designed specifically for churches, but many of the principles are useful. It touches upon areas like copyright consideration that other books of this sort do not.

Cheney, Theodore A. Rees. *Writing Creative Nonfiction*. Berkeley, Calif: Ten Speed Press, 1991.

This book explains the process of writing and how it is done. It shows how to write gripping lead sentences and how to create excitement through prose. It is easy reading.

Crowder, Robert G. and Richard K. Wagner. *The Psychology of Reading*. New York: Oxford University Press, 1992.

This book provides a psychological study of the process of reading. It gives background information that explains how the process works. This material is useful for understanding why one format is easier to read than another, but it is difficult reading.

Fisher, Robert W. *How to Publish a Near Perfect Newsletter*. North Canton, Ohio: Communication Resources Inc., 1992.

This handbook is a good resource for those who are committed to producing better newsletters. It has a number of suggestions and ideas to improve what is already being done. It also has some excellent surveys for getting information and rating your newsletter.

Gill, Bob. *Forget All The Rules You Ever Learned About Graphic Design Including The Ones In This Book*. New York: Watson-Guptill, 1981.

This is one of the basic graphic design books used by professionals. It explains design theory and offers a visual look at how professionals put theory into practice.

Hurlburt, Allen. *The Design Concept*. New York: Watson-Guptill, 1981.

This book is another of the classics. It is easy reading and filled with examples of good, attention-grabbing design.

Marius, Richard. *A Writer's Companion*. New York: McGraw-Hill Inc., 1991.

A basic book that explains the rules of good writing, this volume discusses everything from writing sentences to essays and arguments.

Parker, Roger C. *Looking Good In Print*. Chapel Hill, N.C.: Ventana Press, 1990.

This is a good handbook on desktop publishing design and layout. Illustrated and very easy to read, it is one of the best books on basic newsletter design concepts.

Parker, Roger C. *Newsletters From The Desktop*. Chapel Hill, NC: Ventana Press, 1990.

This book is quickly becoming a classic with its hands-on approach to producing newsletters. It is aimed at the more professional editor, but the basics are applicable to any newsletter producer. There are lots of examples to look at and to draw ideas from.

York, Yvon. *The Desktop Publishing Remedy*. Elgin, Ill.: David C. Cook Publishing Co., 1993.

A good handbook for those getting acquainted with computers in the church. The book explores what a computer is and especially how it can be used in the church's publishing ministry.